A Time of Cicadas

Elfreida Read

ISBN 0 88750 756 5 (hardcover)
ISBN 0 88750 757 3 (softcover)

Book design by Michael Macklem

Printed in Canada

PUBLISHED IN CANADA BY OBERON PRESS

To Jeani and to Phil, because it is so important to share your heart with your children.

Chapter One

Once there was a city, a city like no other—imperious, ambitious, wicked, cradling affluence and need, culture and ignorance, beauty and ugliness, and unreasonably, painfully, incurably romantic. A city that sprang from mud like a rare, exotic flower, flourished, and died of its own inborn poisons. A city that was built within a fragile shell of opportunity, hope and greed and magic. But the shell cracked and fell apart, its essence drained and all its substance vanished as if it had never been. A Camelot. Shanghai.

It had packed streets and sky-challenging mansions and lice-ridden shacks. In the summer it had flies and mosquitoes and bats, and cockroaches the size of bats, and cicadas chorused all day and frogs at night, the hoarse, dry, invincible voices of the tropics. It had cold winters with bone-cracking winds from Mongolia, springs full of lilac and wisteria and magnolia blossoms, and autumns redolent with roasting chestnuts and wildly luxuriant with cosmos. On the famous Bund there was a famous club that boasted the longest bar in cocktail history, and the city had theatres offering operas and symphonies—and it had opium dens. Flags from all the sea-going countries in the world decked the ships moored at the Bund in what surely was the dirtiest river ever to lap around their flanks. And the outline of a junk's sails at sunset crushed your heart.

This was my city, my Camelot, the city that sprang from the mud and flourished, and then was lost in time, leaving behind it only the husks of its glamour. And this is the reason why I want to tell you what it was like when I was young and walked under those Far Eastern skies. I want to do this because you will never be able to go there yourself, any more than you can step at will into the substance and memories of those who lived there for that short enchanted time.

I would like to recall for you how we sat on wide verandahs on sweltering summer afternoons, the women decked out in voile or georgette, or later in trendy seersucker, the dresses sticking to their backs, and the men's short-sleeved, cotton shirts always damp about the armpits, sipping tea and listening to the cicadas sawing in the treetops. How we watched the proud, grand steamers sliding smoothly into dock to the endless refrain of chanting coolies at the wharf-sides, flanked by raggedy-sailed junks and cheeky little sampans. How we revelled in the magnolia blossoms in the spring and dreaded the approach of dysentery and malaria and cholera. How we walked through streets full of persons of an alien race, yellow-skinned and sloe-eyed, and considered them only a backdrop to our own superior status, even though the land was theirs.

My family was pillared by strong women. I do not know whether I could be construed as one. Fear, anxiety, heartache for my loved ones, discontent with the world are too often with me. Risk-taking is not characteristic, strange dogs frighten me. But there is a strength of hope and purpose and affirmation that is like a rock lodged under my heart, a gut-deep resistance to adversity. This obdurate core is a legacy bequeathed to me by the women of my family and has served me well in exigencies.

Every life demands a centrality. My struggle for such a centrality extended over a period of many years. My spiritual hunger longed for assuagement but I did not know how to satisfy it. It was a long time before I even recognized it for what it was. The kaleidoscopic nature of the city offered a host of spiritual panaceas, each contradicting its rivals, all placebos at best. All around me contending elements angled for possession of my unwary soul. It is these elements I would like to explore.

Today I am present at a celebration. The occasion is the Russian Orthodox Easter, the place is my cousin Nina's condo in the city of Vancouver. I am in the kitchen with my

93-year-old aunt, my Aunt Lena. As always, she is speaking to me in Russian. Mine is getting rusty and I sometimes put in English words into a Russian conversation like stray raisins in a loaf of plain bread. She is saying, "Nyet, nyet, nyet..." I am looking for teaspoons in the wrong drawer of the crowded kitchen. "I'll find them myself," she says, "go and sit down. Have a rest." She is one of those women with that power under her ribs. She glances distrustfully at the electric kettle bubbling gently on the stove. There are two kettles on the stove. One is her tried and true aluminum one, her favourite, even though it has lost its shine and has acquired a few dents. But this is a large family gathering and we are all heavy tea-drinkers, so the electric kettle has been taken out of storage. My aunt's lower lip protrudes a little. A sign of scorn. Scorn for the electric kettle. An upstart invention. Nothing wrong with a plain old kettle. She is matching cups to saucers on the counter, crowded with after-dinner debris. She is tiny, Dresden-delicate, her arms brittle as breadsticks. "Go and have a rest," she repeats. She doesn't like us in her kitchen but is too polite to say so.

I catch Nicholas' eye and laughter trembles between us. "She hates that kettle," I say, taking unfair advantage of her deafness and her inability to catch our quick exchanges in English. "She considers it as some kind of affront. I bet she'll turn it off as soon as we go." He gives in to his laugh, it's an irresistible bray. He is her grandson, my cousin Nina's son. The old lady is always a source of amusement to him as well as some awe and much astonishment. Because of his fondness for her, he handles her whims with grace and skill. He has inherited her high cheekbones and her thin-ridged, lightly aquiline nose, an elegant face. They are both highly intelligent, secretive and determined. She would happily die for him, but between them there is the endless tug-o'-war of the generations. And she still hangs on to her end of the rope, to that power, with amazing tenacity.

She has put tea-leaves into the pot, the best Earl Grey,

and now prepares to add the hot water.

"Let me do it," I offer at once.

"Nyet, nyet, nyet," she says, "I'll do it myself." She tries to lift the electric kettle. It is too heavy. She fails. "Oh, all right then, you do it," she says. "It's this kettle," she adds, "the handle is awkward. I can lift other things perfectly well."

"I know," I say. Her little defeat beats at me painfully. I pour the water into the teapot and change the subject quickly. Nicholas has not failed to notice the small crisis. His eyes are watchful.

We have all come together in this luxurious Shaughnessy condo in Vancouver to celebrate her orthodox Easter. She married a Russian 70 years ago in Vladivostok and embraced his country and his religion. She was born Estonian and a Lutheran, a sister to my mother, but she has carried the torch for old Russia and for the Russian Orthodox Church for as many years as she has scorned upstart new inventions like electric appliances. In their hospitals, she tells us, they did everything the old-fashioned way and no-one ever died. Not unless their time had come, she always adds shrewdly. Her Russian husband was a doctor, she a nurse. His name was Nicholas too. In old, old Russia.

I look at her now, pouring out tea with a slightly shaky hand into the fragile, flowered cups. She has lived for nearly a century. She is one of the last windows on to that century, and when you draw open the drapes and peer out the scene is dimming fast. You have to be quick to catch the remaining light, to make out landscapes, objects, people. People, she has known so many, loved some, wondered at others, disliked a few. "They are all dead," she often says. "I am the last."

She means the last of her generation. We, the next generation, seem to her to live in another world, and as for our children, like Nicholas, they are totally incomprehensible to her. Her world is receding, sucked fast into the maw of the past, but to her it is still the only worthwhile world, the only real one. "Nobody *cares* any more," she often says. "We used to *care.*"

She cares about us. She and my cousin, Nina, have produced a magnificent feast for this most joyful of days in the Russian liturgical calendar. The grandchildren are there, Nicholas, and Alisha, thin-faced, with a Romany allure, quick with explanations, tumbling tales, large eyes dark, defensive, defiant perhaps; a grandniece and nephew, these my own two, sparkling, loquacious Jeani, scattering cigarette ashes and fragments of her eager heart wherever she goes, and Phil, following in a line of fine-looking males, but wary, brooding on the pitfalls of life. There are also the four ancients. These are all women who have survived their spouses, living proof of the durability of the female sex. Their venerable ages add up to well over three hundred. They are weighty, slow-moving, like dirigibles, but alert, interested. They discuss the recent election, the rising prices, their travels, and over and over again the comparative merits of the famous "koolich" and "paskha," the inescapable and incomparable dessert served at every orthodox Easter gathering. Always the one currently being consumed is declared indisputably the best.

A koolich is a cross between bread and cake. It is baked in a tall, round tin and when detinned it stands about a foot and a half high. Paskha, its inseparable companion, is a concoction of cottage cheese and sour cream and butter. It is produced in the shape of a pyramid after a sojourn of several days in a wooden mould in the fridge. The letters XB are deeply impressed into its sides. XB (H and V in the Cyrillic alphabet) stand for Khristos voskrese—Christ is risen. In the old days, and long ago in Russia, each koolich was topped with a special decorator napkin, linen, heavy with icing and sprinkled with coloured sugar. Today the two koolichee stand free of decorations, a small concession to change that has made the right topping unavailable. An era is passing, but my aunt is implacable. "Christ is risen," she says, Easter after Easter, kissing the arriving guests three times on alternate cheeks. "Truly risen," reply the guests in the ancient ritual, returning the kisses.

We have finished dinner. The leftovers of the ham and the turkey and the marinated fish, the mushrooms drowned in rich white sauce, the perky devilled eggs, the jaunty, colourful salads, have all been stowed away in the fridge. Both my aunt and Nina are magnificent cooks. There are always large quantities of leftovers. It would never do to have a shortage. Everyone must be served to the bursting point. The young people sit in a circle on the pale gold carpet, some smoking or indulging in another drink, ribbing each other, laughing, always laughing, even sombre Phil has lightened up, flashing white teeth in racy retorts. My aunt is baffled by them, but she loves them unreservedly. She does not approve of their habits and is anxious about possible spillages, burns—I know that before she goes to bed she will ransack the whole living-room for smouldering butts. "How can they sit on the *floor*?" she asks me in wonderment.

We have served the tea and slices of koolich and paskha, and my cousin, Nina, and I are trying to make some kind of sense out of the chaos in the kitchen. Nina is loading the dishwasher. "She still won't use it, you know," she says, referring to the old lady and to her scorn of modern appliances. "She thinks she does a better job herself." She shakes her head. She has had to put up with a lot. Life presented many pitfalls for Nina. She was stunningly handsome once, and although age and illness have now exacted some of their toll they have not triumphed. On good days, the old queenliness still surfaces, that essence of true quality, impossible to simulate.

She puts a serving-dish into the dishwasher and sighs. She has become heavier with time, my cousin, who once was as slim as a willow-wand. Arthritis has stiffened her limbs. I think of her as she was 40 years ago, straight, slender, dark-haired, milky-skinned, sporting one of those huge hats that were made specially for her by a private milliner, furs over her shoulders. No Greenpeace worries then. She wore sables, minks. Times have changed. Now she sports a "Ban Leghold Traps" sticker on her car bumper.

My first memory of Nina is when I was five years old. She is eight. We are living in Shanghai, my Camelot. The Old Shanghai it is now called, the Shanghai of foreign settlements, concessions, exploitation, wars, opium trading, callousness, poverty, dirt, disease and incredible wealth. A notorious city. But also the Shanghai of glamour and romance. Even the sea smelled differently on out trips to the Pangtsze Delta. It smelled like a sea of enchantment, of unknown adventures and destinations—salty, fresh, full of wide winds and deep blue mysteries.

Nina and I are walking home from her school, chaperoned by my mother. Nina wants some mandarin oranges. My mother buys a bagful. Nina carries them. She's a cute little girl. Slightly pouty-mouthed, petulant perhaps. I have many photographs. Black curly hair held with a bow at the top of her head, the hair at the back allowed to fall free in the style of the day. A hat bounces against her back suspended by an elastic band. She swings the bag of oranges up and down, back and forth, faster and faster. My mother issues a warning. My mother, in her early forties, is a gentle-faced, charming woman. She, together with the other women of her generation, has recently been liberated from the long skirts of her youth. Her brown hair is still piled high on her head. She had not adopted all the styles of the early twenties. Later she will have it marcel-waved. She wears a summer hat, perched high on all that hair, a protection against the scorching Shanghai suns. She rebukes Nina.

"You'll drop those oranges," she says. I say nothing. I shrink from confrontations. But Nina laughs. Alas, that laugh. It comes tumbling across the years, Nina's laugh.

Just before the moment of disaster. For of course the bag bursts and the oranges scatter far and wide.

We know we have lost the oranges. On a Shanghai street dropped objects are seldom retrieved. Even gloves, trinkets or change are often abandoned. Anything retrieved has to be disinfected. And you certainly never pick up any food. Spittle and garbage abound. The Chinese do not use handkerchiefs. They cough and spit freely. Many have dread diseases. We do not pick up the oranges.

A subdued and chastened Nina walks home, glancing over her shoulder at the Chinese children who rush to pick up the fruit. They peel the oranges quickly, stuffing them into their mouths. I can taste the lost sweetness. But I say nothing to Nina. Somehow I know she is ashamed, heartbroken. I never quarrel with Nina.

Shanghai. What were we doing in Shanghai, the two small girls in their kneesocks and shiny buttoned shoes, and their straw hats bobbing around their shoulders? ("Put on your hat," I hear my mother say, "you'll get sunstroke, then you'll be sorry.") We were among the first victims of the great mass migrations that plagued this century and have changed the course of so many histories, the migrations that were responsible for such groups as the one assembled in Nina's condo, emigrants thrown together in an alien land. Today we feel fortunate. We have survived as a family. We have raised the Pepsi generation. But the wars and revolutions are not far behind us, persecution, terror, flight still shadow our dreams. They have bred nostalgia, the wells of bitterness and hate have not dried up.

The tea has been drunk, but there have to be refills, even if only half cups, and always the pressure to eat just a bite more. It is the Russian way. It wouldn't be hospitable not to press. The refusals are overcome, the guests surrender. The young people groan about their violated diets. Conversation flows in two streams. One stream eddies around the Pepsi generation on the carpet, the other, more sober, circles above. This one has now taken a serious hold on the past. "Do you remember," says one of the aged ladies, "the wonderful cakes at the Café Federal?"

"Do I remember them," says another ancient. Her hands are disfigured by arthritis and she holds her cup of tea gingerly, watched anxiously, if covertly, by my aunt who is mindful of the pale gold carpet. "I used to drool when I walked past that place. The chocolates, the meringues, the whipping cream. The cakes layered with chestnut stuffing." She shakes her head.

"There has never been anything like it since," says a third ancient. She is lame and walks with a crutch, but her eyes light with an unearthly glow at the memory.

"Nor ever will be again most likely," says the fourth. She is purblind and always the saddest. "But don't you think it might have only seemed so good because we were young?" And we are all plunged into another world, a world so different from that of the youngsters at our feet that my heart breaks on the sharp edge of the chasm between us.

Chapter Two

I look around. I'm sitting in a half-way house between the old and the new—this coterie, nibbling, sipping, laughing, reminiscing, teasing, perched up in a fancy condo, this coterie—and the ghosts. Oh yes, the ghosts. They are all here with us, moving among us, unseen, unheard, but most certainly there. The ghosts who have been instrumental in bringing us together. Let me tell you that my cousin Nina has even seen them. Nina is a Pisces, and she has seen the ghosts. Sometimes they are sad, grey, sometimes happy, brightly dressed, and sometimes shadowy, indistinct. Once upon a Christmas day, when we were working a ouija board, all of us nervous, laughing overmuch, Nina saw the ghost of St. Matthew. She knew it was St. Matthew as surely as if he had announced himself. That sobered us.

The ghosts sit around us in the fancy condo and they reach back into the disregarded past and draw it forward into the living present.

"I admire your aunt so much," says a guest sitting next to me, one of Nina's co-workers at the college where she teaches. We watch Aunt Lena as she walks carefully across the pale gold carpet with yet another cup of tea for one of the four ancients trembling a little in her withered-petal hands. "You say she is the last of her generation. How many were there in her family? I'd love to know more about them all."

How the ghosts rustle. What a stirring they're making. Each one eager to be remembered, appreciated, prized. Tell about me, tell about me.

"There were four sisters and three brothers," I begin, and then fall silent. There is so much to say it seems futile even to begin.

"What was the Café Federal?" asks the guest, curious, puzzled by my silence.

"It was simply a very good bakery," I say. But that isn't the whole truth. I think about it, smiling a bit. How can I explain something like that? The Café Federal was a symbol. A highwater mark. If you shopped at the Café Federal you had arrived. You had made your niche, dug in your heels, put it any way you like. You were in Shanghai to stay. When you paid your money and took the cake box from across the counter there was no doubt about the future of the International Settlement. It would be there forever, and so would you.

The Café Federal was situated in the heart of the Settlement, in the district of the Shanghai well-to-do, on the famous Bubbling Well Road. When I was older and we lived on a street called Avenue Haig, on the border of the French Concession, my mother and I would often walk down to have tea with my Aunt Lena who lived on Bubbling Well Road, close to the Café Federal. It was about a twenty-minute walk. We first passed scores of Chinese stores with bizarre banners advertising wares in hieroglyphics I never learned to understand because nobody thought it was important to learn the Chinese language. We threw coppers to our favourite beggars, the dwarf, the cheerful legless one who swung his torso on his arms supported by two wooden handrests, the blind one, who rattled chopsticks in an empty bowl. My mother told me that she had once seen him studying a coin when he thought no-one was watching, but she still gave him something because she thought he looked like a sage. Perhaps he was a rascal, she said, but he was certainly a sharp-witted one. And she laughed and shrugged in that charming manner she had. As we walked toward my aunt's house, the streets began to change in character. They became westernized. We were approaching the heart of the Settlement. The stores were clean and modern and their names were carried only in English. We passed large apartment houses in private compounds. Just before we reached my aunt's apartment we passed by the Café Federal.

Yes, as the weighty ancient had said, it had all those magnificent cakes in the window, chocolate and whipped cream and meringues, nuts and fruit and pastries galore with dustings of icing sugar, I could only dream of such dainties in my everyday life. But I knew that on the great Russian holidays, Christmas and Easter, and on the name's-days of the holy saints, some of those cakes and a variety of pastries would find their way to my Aunt Lena's house, to her sumptuously provided table, and I could indulge. By then my Aunt Lena was well-to-do.

During those years, as I grew from a chunky little girl into a lanky teenager, my Aunt Lena and her Russian doctor had established themselves in the alien, uncaring city, and had prospered. "Nina's parents did well in Shanghai," I say to the guest at the Easter party. "Her father was a very clever doctor. In those days doctors really had to live by their wits, they didn't have stacks of handy medications to depend on. And my Aunt Lena coped with everything else."

"I can believe that," says the guest, "but how did you all get there? Why Shanghai?"

"It all started so very long ago," I say, glancing at my aunt who is shaking her head at some ribaldry from the crew sitting on the carpet. Her hair has become so thin she wears a neat, close-fitting grey wig. It suits her well and keeps her head warm. "It was a large family," I say. "They lived in Kronstadt, which is close to Leningrad, except then it was called Petrograd, and once St. Petersburg of course. My aunt still calls it Petrograd, and sometimes even Petersburg. She never, never calls it Leningrad." I ponder this strange fact for a few moments and then continue.

"My grandfather was an official in the courts and they were well off. They had a spacious apartment with a cook and a maid. My aunt remembers how they all used to sit around the large dining-room table evening after evening, under an oil lamp, the children with their homework, the father with his law books, the mother sewing. Best of all she remembers how very peaceful it was. How safe." Someone calls to the guest across the room, and the subject changes. We lose the thread. But the ghosts have positioned themselves around me and I slip out to the patio and lean on the rail in the quiet night away from the noise of the party, and continue to muse.

Discipline ruled that home. Love was unquestioned but seldom mentioned. Sex and politics never. Perhaps the father was aware that events were forming, shaping invisibly like deadly fumes, events that threatened his family, but it is unlikely that even he could have guessed then how far-reaching those events would be, how they would break up

My grandfather

Alexander's fiancée, my mother, Alexander, Ernest, my grandmother

that peaceful home, that close-knit group, and scatter them around the globe, some never to see one another again. Perhaps he had qualms, but certainly no-one else in the family gave a thought to anything like that.

A family of eight, gathered around an oil-lamp in a warm dining-room, at peace. One of those children was my mother. The youngest of the girls was my Aunt Lena. There were two more girls and two boys. Another boy was to be born several years later, a surprise, and was to play a strangely divisive role in the family, not at all compatible with his good looks and cheerful temperament, my Uncle Ernest.

Their lives were uneventful. Excitement was provided by skating parties in the winter with lanterns strung under the stars and Straus waltzes delighting the participants, and in the summer by a holiday to the farm of the paternal grandfather. This patriarch had an underground ice cellar and took his own potatoes with him whenever he was invited out to dinner to the ineffable embarrassment of the paternal grandmother. Later, when the girls grew to be older they were taken to Petrograd to an occasional concert or opera. They would ride to the city across the frozen inlet in a sleigh filled with blankets and straw and come home under a brilliant moon that turned their whole world into a fairyland. Once my Aunt Lena fell out of the sleigh and no-one noticed until the sleigh was half way across the inlet. Outings like that were privileges to be earned by good behaviour and that was mandatory. Punishment for disobedience was a birching with a bundle of twigs against a bare backside. Girls were not exempt, but the mere threat of the trouncing was enough to keep them in line. All four girls were singularly well-favoured. No-one had any doubts that they would all marry, and marry well. The older ones began to plan their trousseaus early.

Time was silk slipping between careless fingers. Their lives moved through an eternal summer of the soul. They were aware that somewhere, beyond the boundaries of their well-ordered lives, there were The Poor. But they did not think about them. They were part of that outside world, something as inevitable as rain or winter storms, and something you could conveniently put out of your mind much as you could forget bad weather in a comfortable room. The mother contributed to an old people's home, a charitable institution, and Aunt Lena and my mother were delegated every Sunday to walk to this home with a basket of goodies for a retired female servant. The country road seemed endless for they longed to get back to Sunday pleasures, visits and visitors, games, gossip and girlish pursuits and diversions. But go they had to. I can see them, two attractive young girls in long skirts and buttoned up boots, their Sunday hats beflowered and beribboned, trudging, begrudgingly, to deliver their gifts.

The eldest boy Alexander, was a paragon. He was the idol of the four girls. Good-looking, brilliant, gracious, there was no end to his virtues. He entered the military academy in Petrograd and graduated, an officer in the Tsar's army with the highest honours. I have a picture of him, his hair, curiously, a brushcut not too different from the cuts of the late fifties, handsome indeed in his uniform, double-breasted with brass buttons and epaulettes. So young. Sometimes I hold the picture in my hands and look long into the serious face. An ancestor. Once a person of blood and bone, a person my mother knew intimately, had hugged, admired, adored, perhaps of whose affections and attentions she was jealous, with whom she undoubtedly occasionally quarrelled. A real person, now only a fading photograph. Someone I had never seen, and yet the same blood ran through his veins as now courses through mine.

I also have a picture of the second brother, Vladimir. He was not a family favourite. Dark and somewhat morose, he has fine eyes and a defiant stare. Reports about him have come down via the family grapevine. He hated school, played truant, was often birched. Whenever I hold the two pictures side by side, I turn against the star, Alexander. My sympathies are with Vladimir. I recognize the rancour already in the soul of this less than favourite son. There too I can feel the tug of blood and somehow in his case the ties are closer, warmer, more immediate—Vladimir, the rebel, the school dropout of a former day, who later apprenticed himself to a shoemaker and kept the entire family in bread during the worst years of the revolution.

The four sisters merge in my mind. They are like four flowers born of a parent stem, often blown apart by the wind and yet always pulling together again, lifting their heads side by side to face the elements, sometimes almost indeed as if they were one flower. They presented a strong united front. They had a startling family resemblance. Yet their personalities differed widely and were clearly defined.

The eldest, the full-bosomed and beautiful Lila, I never knew. She was torn away from that stem and later undoubtedly perished in the bombing of Warsaw where she had gone with her husband, but strangely she never really seemed to have left the foursome. They spoke of her as if she were still there, as if she had just left the house, perhaps for a shopping jaunt, and would return at any moment, so that I too considered her as present, albeit somehow invisible, an inalienable part of the whole, a buxom ghost.

Aunt Lila has come down to me as proud and luxury-loving. In the photographs I have she wears thick furs and heavy jewellery, bracelets, rings, chains. She seems to say that it is the right of women to be admired and pampered. By contrast the second sister, Lydia, my Aunt Lida, was modest, industrious, secretive and vulnerable. She took a back seat, had no inflated opinions of herself, and was happy when she was of use to others. My mother, third down the line, Maria, or Manya as the sisters called her, was light-hearted and endowed with that gift for humour that stood her in such good stead when disasters struck one after another. My mother's answer to most difficulties was a shrug and a quip. And my Aunt Lena, Elena the youngest, now ministering to the guests at the condo, was strong-minded, independent and self-motivated. It was she who caused the memorable uproar in the family when, at the age of seventeen, she decided to become a nurse, outraging my staid Kronstadt grandfather. It took all my grandmother's skill and diplomacy to prevent a major rift. My grandfather was convinced that women who sought a career and independence like the English suffragettes were either communists or prostitutes, and often both. My grandmother, secretly on the side of the suffragettes, tried to persuade him otherwise. The drama raged for months in the quiet Kronstadt home, until, with the advice of a friendly neighbourhood doctor who promised to keep an eye on the aspiring crusader, the father capitulated. Aunt Lena had her way.

These were the people who formed the backdrop of my life on my mother's side. The first intimation that life was not just one long endless summer of the soul came to them early. My mother was 22, in love, heart light as air, when my grandfather announced that he was being transferred from Kronstadt to Vladivostok. He was in line for a judgeship. It was a big promotion.

Vladivostok. The other end of the world.

There was no question of course but that they had to go. It did not matter that my grandmother had to pull up ancient roots, abandon her parents, her friends of a lifetime, that the girls had to leave their sweethearts behind, jettison their pals, relinquish everything they knew and loved. Grandfather's career came first, as it always did with men. I think Vladimir, the rebel, was the only one who welcomed the move. It promised change and adventure and an escape from the ambience of the perfect Alexander who was to remain behind at his post, for he was already an officer.

The journey across the Russian steppes took close to three weeks. At every station the train crew jumped out to chop down trees and prepare logs to feed the engine. The family ate at restaurants at each stop, or bought food from the peasants who set up stalls offering tantalizing concoctions. The mother was suspicious of these delicacies. The peasants were stupid, the mother said, they knew nothing of cleanliness, they were just *peasants,* the restaurants were more reliable, but the girls pleaded, and if the food was steaming hot she would relent and allow them to buy it, the piroshkee cooked in boiling fat, cups of scalding borsch, pirogee with mouth-watering fillings. The peasant women bobbed their thanks, the men doffed their caps to the wealthy travellers. Little did the travellers know how soon the days of bobbing and cap-doffing would be over. The pitchforks they saw held no menace.

My Uncle Ernest was on that trek, the youngest son born so much later. A child of three or four, blue eyes, gold curls, already learning to depend on the adoration of women. All the sisters were mothers to him.

So they arrived in Vladivostok and settled. They lived in an exclusive district. They had servants, clothes, jewels, a sumptuous table. The four girls resigned themselves to the change of scene. Aunt Lena immediately went to work for the naval hospital. She had opened the way for the other sisters. Office jobs were being offered to women and Aunt Lila and Aunt Lida both found employment despite deep-seated rumbles from my grandfather. My mother alone remained at home to help my grandmother run the household.

She and my Aunt Lida were the two who had left sweethearts behind in Kronstadt. The eldest, Lila, had formed no such attachment so she had no problems rearranging her life. At her office she met a Pole and in no time she had married him. Poles were held in some disfavour by the Russians, but not by Estonians. He was well off and it was he who took my beautiful aunt to Warsaw in the early twenties. After the Second World War we never heard from them again.

Aunt Lida never married. She remained tragically faithful

to her first love. Faithful till she died in a Vancouver hospital in her eighties. Aunt Lena met her Russian doctor in the hospital where she was working and her future was instantly established. And my mother scuttled her first romance and married my father, Albert Ennock.

He was a business executive engaged in the merchandising of specialized books. He was well off, with excellent prospects. In 1912 the ordinary citizen did not think of revolutions, especially not in an outpost like Vladivostok. My father was also Estonian. A pleasant man, on the homely side, but kind, and an intellectual, a good catch, even though he was much older than my mother. I have a picture of my mother taken just before the wedding. She is enchantingly pretty. She wears a form-fitting gown and a large hat piled with ruffles. Her features are small, classical. Hair in a roll, high under the hat. She could have been an actress, she was so lively and quick-tongued, but such an idea was unthinkable. There were limits to my grandfather's concessions. In the picture she holds herself with grace, pride. She wears a small locket round her neck. It was a locket given to her by the sweetheart in Kronstadt before she left. He had promised to follow her. I do not think my mother ever wore that locket after she married my father. Gold, lozenge-shaped, set with ruby and diamond chips, it is now my daughter's prized possession.

My mother did not marry my father for love. She respected him and no doubt grew to love him. But she never failed to make it clear to him that she was not in love with him. I do not know why she felt obliged to dwell on this hurtful fact. It was a small enough touch of cruelty, perhaps traceable to the heartache for her lost love, but cruelty that I resented. Later I came to see it as a protective measure. She was not going to have her heart broken again. Nonetheless, my father adored her. He was going to make a paradise for her.

Their home when they first married was elegant. My

mother had fine linens, handsome tableware and six potted palms in her dining-room. I have a yellowed picture of that dining-room with its windows soaring to the ceiling, shrouded in heavy lace. My mother sits at the head of the table. Her hair is drawn back and arranged in a bouffant, caught up in a net at the nape of her neck in the style of the day. She is heart-catchingly young. There is a large samovar on the table, the samovar that travelled with her later to Shanghai. There are cups, liqueur bottles and glasses, flowers. And around the room are the six palms, towering over the guests. My father is looking at my mother with his face full of tenderness. I often saw that look in later years. There had been servants and a club where they were served caviar and oysters and champagne, where they had often danced till dawn. There was a charming little girl, my sister Irene, her clothes weighted with laces, bows in her hair, sporting white boots and patent leather shoes. But this paradise was short-lived.

The revolution started before I was born, in 1917, but its reverberations took some time to reach the Far East. They arrived about the same time as my mother became pregnant with me. Everyone advised an abortion. It could be done safely, medical advice was available. Another child in the family when the whole world was collapsing around them was sheer lunacy. Another mouth to feed when they were already standing in queues for the barest necessities. But my mother held out. "God gave me this child," she is reported to have said, histrionically, somehow by-passing Father, "and God will provide." And, miraculously, He did.

The revolution reached Vladivostok and my Aunt Lena and her doctor were advised to leave immediately. He was a medical officer in the Tsar's navy. The sailors were getting nasty. But leaving required money. The banks had crashed, their savings were gone. Here Aunt Lena sprang a surprise. Several years before, on their honeymoon, the doctor had given her a generous sum to spend on herself, on whatever caught her fancy. The honeymoon was on board the naval ship and they visited Japan, Saigon, Shanghai, names full of mystery and romance, distant, alien. She had played with the idea of making some special purchase, but there was nothing she wanted. Love was enough. Once home she had hidden the money and now, to everyone's astonishment, she brought it out. It was enough for the journey.

They left as soon as possible. Even then it was almost too late. Sailors, liberated by the revolution, came storming to the docks when they found out that the ship was about to sail with the white officers on board, but the vessel managed to cast off before the sailors could board.

So they sailed, packed into the hold, Aunt Lena, her Russian doctor and my cousin Nina. Behind them they left the family who were not in any serious danger because they were Estonians and now liberated from Russian domination. However, conditions were execrable and my father too began to consider leaving. Aunt Lila and her Pole were childless and Aunt Lida unmarried, as was Vladimir, but my father had two small children to think about. Food was short, there was plague in the poorer quarters of the city. My mother vacillated. Then one day as she and Aunt Lida walked home with a Chinese carrier behind them lugging the groceries they had collected by standing in several tedious queues, the carrier dropped to the ground. He had the plague. They fled, leaving the groceries behind. It seemed to be the final straw for which my mother had been waiting. That evening she and my father made the decision to go.

The new government made no attempt to stop them, but they were allowed to take with them only their personal possessions, and those to a prescribed limit, and twelve pounds of silver. My mother took her wedding gifts and her samovar. My father packed his encyclopaedia, a set of twelve volumes, sacrificing precious luggage space for what he valued most, the conservation of knowledge.

Chapter Three

We travelled by train. I remember the journey as long and full of curious fears. There was a conductor who took my teddy bear and tossed him up to the light in our compartment and my three-year-old heart was filled with sharp anxiety for the fate of my beloved toy. The overpowering might of the train as it tore along its rails alarmed me so much that I refused to get off my seat in case the compartment and all I loved rushed away without me, leaving me alone in the bleak, strange countryside. I remember a shabby, echoing hotel-room with a very high ceiling and a black sink in one corner with rusty taps. I cried when my well-meaning sister, then eleven, washed my hands in that sink. It often visits me in my dreams, gaping, sinister, emblematic of the sad, disquieting journey. All my first memories are of travel and fear.

But in spite of all these hazards we arrived in Shanghai safely. My parents were hardly able to believe that their world had crumbled. Behind them the empire of the Tsar was dissolving like a mud-pie on a rainy day. Their immediate prospects were poor. My father was over 50 when he found himself with a wife and two small girls in the lap of a Chinese city indifferent to his plight and monopolized by foreign interests for whom money was the sole arbiter. He felt fortunate to get a job with a Swiss firm where his fluency in five languages was useful, but they knew he was disadvantaged and they exploited him. At the start his wage was barely enough for comfortable living and he worked week after week from Monday through Saturday and never had a longer holiday than an extra day at Christmas.

We first lived with my Aunt Lena, her Russian doctor husband and my cousin Nina, in a small terrace house in the French Concession. We had the attic. It was a poky place with little light. I slept in a roomy crib, with pink iron rails and grey netting, bought at an auction. My sister thought I was too big for a crib but my mother said the size and price were right. My constant activity on the uncarpeted floor and stairs disturbed my uncle administering to his patients below, so my mother made me my first pair of slippers. They were padded. I remember the soft spongy give in the soles of those slippers and how delighted I was with them. I was not told the real reason for the slippers until years later. My aunt had not wanted to hurt my feelings, to make me feel that I was a source of annoyance. It was my first encounter with the blight that marred the otherwise felicitous life of that little family—my doctor uncle suffered from frequent and severe migraines and my Aunt Lena did her devoted best to mitigate situations that might trigger an attack. It must have been trying for my aunt to have a family of four move in on her, but she never showed it.

In that first home in Shanghai, crowded and shadowy, my cousin had measles and had to lie in bed with a red shade over her lamp and heavy drapes across the windows to protect her eyes. In the summer my sister came home for the holidays. She had been placed in an English boarding-school at the other end of the city so that she could learn the new language among her peers. I remember a great thunderstorm and my sister inciting my cousin and me to taunt the thunder at the open door and then to dive under the dining-room table at each house-shaking peal. "Thunder, thunder, we're here down under, but we're not afraid of you!" we sang, but I *was* afraid. The next day we went to see a great tree riven by lightning and we knew that nature was not to be taunted. I felt guilty about the taunting, as if the death of the tree had been our fault.

It was in this dining-room too that my sister persuaded Nina and me to learn extracts from Shakespeare. She would help me up on to the dining-room table (in my padded slippers) and urge me to recite Mark Anthony's oration. "Friends, Romans, countrymen," I shouted after her delightedly, "lend me your ears." I was Mark Anthony until my aunt appeared in the doorway and swept me off my podium. My aunt's decisiveness and her tight lips awed us all.

At this point the scenario changes. We have moved to a new and larger house. There is a new person in our lives. It is my Uncle Ernest. He is 21 and has recently arrived from Russia. He is brother to my mother and Aunt Lena and my grandparents have decided to send him out of the war-torn country. He has thick, very blond, curly hair and friendly blue eyes. He squats down and talks to me on my own level. "How are you, tovarish," he says in Russian, laughing. My Aunt Lena frowns, I don't know why.

There is an accident. The gas heater explodes in the bathroom. My new uncle's face is strangely flushed. His eyebrows are singed, his blue eyes closed. He is helped to the couch in the sitting-room and my Aunt Lena applies wet cloths to his face and eyes. Anxiety grips me. What will happen to my charming new uncle? But the doctor tells us not to worry. My new uncle will recover. The doctor's voice is quiet and confident, he is kind and reassuring. These qualities, along with the bouts of agony we know he undergoes when migraines strike, have created an attitude among us akin to reverence for him. Later I will remember him standing by my sick-bed, that dark-moustached face full of thought, his hands brought up to his chin, fingers touching lightly as if he were at prayer, a characteristic pose. Perhaps he *was* praying, he was a very religious man. He rarely smiled and his laugh was never hearty, but there was a wealth of caring in his face and concern in the stoop of his shoulders that were more comforting than any levity could have been.

I experience a small triumph. I am walking with my father beside a long, low, stone wall. I climb up on the wall and continue to walk, holding his hand. His hand is warm, protective, large, soft. It is a great adventure to be walking on the wall. I suddenly let go his hand. I can balance on my own. I can run along the wall without falling.

There are fireworks. It is 14 July, Bastille Day, and the French are celebrating. Earlier in the day my sister went to a fair in the French Park. She was the only one allowed to go, Nina and I being deemed too young. When she returned she brought me a tiny porcelain dog not more than an inch and a half long. The tiny dog is white with brown spots and brown ears. I love him more than anything in the world. In the evening we sit on the verandah and watch the fireworks. It's very hot and we all have lemonade as a special treat. Lit mosquito coils send their acrid fumes into the air. I hold the tiny dog in my hand hidden deep in my pocket. Throughout my childhood I will carry him in my pocket wherever I go. I will never lose him.

My sister is preparing a net and a jar. We are going to catch fireflies. At nightfall we go into a mysterious garden full of bushes and trees. We can see the fireflies flitting. My sister nets firefly after firefly. She releases them one by one into the jar slapping the lid on quickly each time. We take the fireflies home. We show the fireflies to Mother but in the lighted room they do not shine. We are disappointed and let them go.

We have moved house again. Now we are no longer sharing a domicile with my aunt. My father has joined the Swiss firm. We can be independent though we are far from rich. We are renting the ground-floor suite in a house on Wayside Road. Wayside Road is at the opposite end of the city from the French Concession and from the new modern cultural centre where the homes of the wealthy are located and where clubs and theatres have sprung up. It is the old end of the city. We are now quite close to my sister's school and she has become a day scholar. Although the basic city requirements have been filled here—paving, lighting, police protection—the streets are narrower, there are fewer trees, everything looks greyer, shabbier, as if this northeastern part of the city lies in perpetual shadow. I feel this but do not reflect upon it. I don't know anything yet about districts or wealth or prestige.

Our suite has two spacious rooms and a kitchen. The house is large with sweeping front steps graced with two enormous stone vases. My sister and I sleep in a curtained-off alcove. The suite is heated by a large black stove set in the centre of the bedroom. The toilet is located outside the suite under the stairs. It has no flush and is carried out every day by a "modoong" amah. The "modoong" amah has a cart with huge containers into one of which she empties the contents of our toilet. This cargo will then be taken to the fields to be used as fertilizer. It is one of the reasons why we can never eat any vegetables raw without disinfecting them.

The "modoong" amah is a strong woman who looks like a man. She even has a moustache. I am terrified of her. One day as I am leaving the toilet I meet the "modoong" amah in the dim recess under the stairs. Her clothes are ragged and soiled, her face is weather-beaten, like wrinkled leather, there is a rag tied round her head. I am paralyzed. After a moment I start to scream. My screams hit the low ceiling and rebound on my ears. My mother comes running. The "modoong" amah laughs and laughs.

We have a boy who helps Mother in the kitchen. One day she catches him skimming the gravy off the pot roast and replacing it with water. She fires him. We get another boy. My mother catches him washing his socks in the basin in which we wash our dishes. She fires him.

My sister has acquired boyfriends. One of them plays "Moonlight and Roses" on his mandolin, sitting on the front steps. English soldiers from the barracks just outside the Settlement come to visit. One of these soldiers is called Vickery. He wears a uniform that smells of wool and leather. He has a bicycle. I long to ride it but it's too high. Vickery steadies the bicycle against the garden gate and lifts me on to it. Only one foot reaches the turned-up pedal. The other hangs free. But I am enchanted. I am in love with Vickery.

In my mind I plan to marry Vickery but a Dutch girl who lives next door, my sister's friend, tells us that she has become engaged to Vickery. I am devastated. I stop speaking to Vickery. I will never ride his silly bicycle again.

One Sunday when my sister and I are making card-houses on the dining-room table the cards keep falling. My sister scolds and tells me to stop shaking the table. I'm not shaking the table I protest, but Mother comes in and sweeps the cards up anyway because it's time for the mid-day meal. We call it tiffin. During tiffin the table shakes again. My father tells me to stop shaking the table. I lose my temper. "I'm *NOT* shaking the table," I shout. The table shakes more than ever. The grownups look at one another with startled faces. It's an earthquake. Later my sister takes me into the garden and shows me deep cracks in the earth where the ground opened up.

Once again we change our quarters. It seems that the landlord wants the suite for himself. We have found attic accommodation on a street called Ward Road. It is opposite the Ward Road Gaol and the police station. I love this attic. It's very large and I have a little alcove all to myself. I have never had any place to myself before. My mother calls it my corner. She says everyone in the world should have a corner of their own. My bed, still my old crib, stands in the alcove. One side of the grey netting is now down permanently because I have grown old enough not to tumble out. I have a black wicker trunk in which I keep my toys. It's my very own trunk. It came with me all the way from Russia. I have acquired a number of dolls and they sit in a row on top of the wicker trunk, together with the teddy bear that was my companion on the train from Vladivostok. On my fifth birthday my parents give me a small wicker table with two chairs and a dolls' tea-set. I couldn't be happier.

We celebrate New Year's Eve on Ward Road. This is a very important occasion in our family. My father has made it so. He always hopes that the year following will be better than the year just past. We are allowed to stay up till midnight and there are cookies, nuts and sweet baked apples to eat, and a glass of wine each. Mine is very small but my mother says it is enough. My sister reads a poem by Tennyson called "The Death of the Old Year." As soon as she begins to read it I begin to weep. "Full knee-deep lies the winter snow," reads my sister, "And the winter winds are wearily sighing. Toll ye the church-bell sad and slow, And tread softly and speak low, For the old year lies a-dying." My weeping grows. I picture the old year as an aged man wrapped in a cloak or blanket and looking a bit like my father. He is dying. I am now weeping without restraint. My mother remonstrates with my sister but my sister says that it's a classic, I must learn it, and reads on relentlessly. When the reading is over we wait in silence as the minutes tick by. "Old year, you must not die; You came to us so readily, You lived with us so steadily, Old Year, you shall not die." But the old year *is* dying. Something momentous is happening. My father takes his watch out of his waistcoat pocket and removes it from the chain that stretches across his belly. He lays the watch on the dining-table. On the wall hang two large calendars, each about a foot square. One loudly proclaims that it is 31 December. The other is mysteriously shrouded by a red cover page. We wait. "Old Year, you shall not die." But you will.

I look at my father. His face, with its broad cheekbones and large nose, is expectant. There is a smile in his eyes as he watches us, amusement, as if he's a conjuror about to perform a magic trick, as if the advent of the new year is his doing. On the table beyond the ticking watch, the cookies and nuts and baked apples, and the four glasses of wine, one very small (but enough), are caught in an enchanted eternity, like objects in a still-life canvas. When the second hand of the watch touches twelve my father says, "Aha!" Simultaneously he rips the last sheet that says 31 December off the old calendar and the cover page off the new one. A large new 1 January 1926 now appears on the wall, and we all shout "Happy New Year!" The old calendar dangles sadly with only a black backsheet showing.

My father takes the old calendar off the wall and throws it into the wastepaper basket. I dwell sadly on the fate of the old year but my sorrow is short-lived for it is now time for the treats. We toast each other with the wine and eat the goodies. Our parents beam at my sister and me. We've all made it into another year. A better year.

We do not live on Ward Road for very long. My mother goes down to visit our landlady one day and finds her dead in her chair by the fireplace. My mother has an anxiety attack and takes valerian drops in half a glass of water. They smell delicious. There is a great commotion. As I am overlooked in the general upset I talk to my dolls about it. They don't know what it means to be dead any more than I do.

I see a coffin moved out of the house into a large car. I have never seen a coffin. It fills me with ineffable horror. I overhear my sister's girlfriend telling her about someone who woke up after he was buried. I live with the terror of being buried alive for years.

The landlady's relatives are taking over the house and we have to find another place to live. We move into a flat in a handsome old house on a street called Baikal Road, but handsome though it may be it is still on the east side of the city.

On Baikal Road we have two bedrooms, a sitting-room and a dining-room with a separate kitchen, unlike the attic where everything was jammed together. I share a room with my sister. She is generous as always and gives me the part under the window. I set up housekeeping with my black wicker trunk, my dolls and my little table and two chairs. My sister gives me two small Japanese dolls. They are about six inches long and have very white clay faces and very black straight hair. They are dressed in red kimonos with a black-

My Uncle Ernest

My sister Irene (holding my hand) and Cousin Nina

and-white design. I love them passionately and keep them on my bed. Later I will introduce them to the other dolls but right now I must have them with me all the time.

A Eurasian family lives next door and the children tease me about a boy who lives down the lane and who comes to visit them. I had foolishly asked his name, thus revealing my interest in him. I am furious at the teasing. I take a terrible revenge. I jump up on the fence between our houses and yell, "*Your* mother is *Chinese*!" They fall silent instantly. They never speak to me again.

In the garden I see a lizard. I am delighted with it. I try to pick it up. The lizard's tail immediately drops off and the lizard and its tail scurry off in different directions. I scurry back to the house in a state of great agitation. Will the lizard ever meet his tail?

On Baikal Road I wake one morning to the most significant day of my life.

I am going to school.

I am going to the same school as my sister. I stand in front of a tall mirror set in the door of a wardrobe. I look splendid. I am dressed in a navy blue uniform, a tunic with wide pleats, a white blouse, a green tie and sash, white socks and, glory of glories, shiny new patent leather shoes. I jump up and down in my shoes. I can't wait to go.

My mother takes me to the school. We travel in a tramcar. At the school she delivers me to the kindergarten teacher and leaves me. The door clicks behind her. I can't believe it. I never thought for a moment that she would leave me. I burst into tears. I weep uncontrollably. My heart is broken. I wet my pants.

In the centre of the kindergarten classroom is a huge black stove surrounded by a black mesh screen. There are wet pants draped over the screen all around the stove. Mine join the rest. I am devastated. I am shamed to the cold little core of my being. The kindergarten teacher is large and warm. Her name is Mrs. Aliston. She takes me on her lap and gives me a hug. I feel better. She picks up a book and shows me a picture of a little girl holding out her hands for a ball. The caption reads, "Alice, catch the ball." It is the first sentence I shall learn to read in English. I shall never forget it.

On the last day of the week I race to meet my mother who has come to fetch me. "I never cried today," I tell her proudly. She praises me.

It is spring. From Baikal Road we travel by tram to visit my Aunt Lena. I am tremendously excited. I love to see my cousin Nina. They have moved out of the terrace house and are now living in an apartment on a street called Carter Road. I am dressed in my best clothes because it is Nina's Easter.

Nina's family celebrates the Russian Orthodox Easter, which falls on a different date from our Lutheran Easter for three consecutive years and coincides on the fourth year. My Aunt Lena says their Easter is the right one because its dates were set before the calendar was changed by Julius Caesar. I am discomfited by this explanation but I don't give it much thought as I am looking forward to all the goodies we are going to have and to the game that Nina and I play whenever I go to visit. Their apartment has a roof garden and the game consists of Nina pushing me around it in a large, black doll's pram. When we're tired of this we push the cat around. He hates it.

Aunt Lena has put up new drapes in the sitting-room of their apartment. They are white and frothy, an expensive tulle. I hear the ladies talking about them. The sun is shining through the frothy material. It lights up the icon set in the corner of the sitting-room and bathes the room in a hallowed milky light. Aunt Lena's home has an icon in every room. The icons are very beautiful, painted in many colours and gilt-edged. Some are of Jesus, and others are of the saints. They are part of my doctor uncle's Russian Orthodox religion.

There are Easter lilies everywhere, drenching the air with

perfume, and of course there is coolich and paskha, the traditional dessert that reaches back through the centuries and will reach forward many years later to a Vancouver condo celebration. A table has been elegantly laid in the dining-room. The tablecloth is of heavy white linen and there is a huge bowl of flowers in the centre. There is also a bowl of coloured eggs set to one side. The silver and the cut glass wink and flash in the afternoon sun. My doctor uncle stands at one end of the table, his hands pointed at his chin, in his customary pose. I don't think he is praying, I think he is just admiring the table. But perhaps he's giving thanks.

Back on Baikal Road our visit fades and Nina's home slips into the fantasy world in which I spend so much of my time. It will emerge again I know, but for the time being it's good to be with my own things again, to tell my dolls about my visit, and to savour each new experience that falls to my lot. At school we are informed that there is to be an eclipse of the sun. I am told that if you look at the sun during an eclipse you will go blind. On the day of the eclipse I don't look out of the window and keep my eyes on the ground when I walk home.

Chapter Four

Louba is a year older than I am and she's very clever. She leads the class in everything. For a reason unclear to me I have been catapulted in a few months through kindergarten and two transition classes into Form One. I don't know anyone in Form One and Louba has made herself responsible for me. I like her very much and am proud that she wants to be friends. Louba explains to me that she is Jewish but the significance of this passes me by. During morning assembly,

Louba and a few other girls leave the assembly hall. This is because we are having prayers and the Jewish girls can't join us. An English girl, called May Davenport, tells me that the Jews killed Jesus and that's why Louba can't stay in the assembly hall when we are having prayers. May says that the Jews are wicked. I don't think Louba is wicked. I think she is pretty and clever.

We have tiffin in the school dining-room. I don't like the meals, they are nothing like my mother's cooking and I pass a lot of my food on to the other children when Matron isn't looking. Louba never eats in the dining-room. She explains to me that she has to eat special Jewish food, that her mother prepares it and she eats it outside on the steps. I wish my mother were Jewish.

One day we are served prunes for dessert. I look at my dish of prunes and see that there is a large black cockroach among the prunes. I call Matron. "There is a cockroach in my prunes," I tell her. "It won't hurt you," Matron says, "it's dead. Just push it aside." I burst into tears and run out of the dining-room.

My mother is summoned to the school. After this I am given sandwiches every morning. I eat my lunch on the steps with Louba and we do our homework together. Louba is generous and helps me whenever I get stuck with anything. She tells me that I'll soon catch up with her and we'll both be top of the class. I doubt it.

My mother becomes friendly with May Davenport's mother. They live quite close to us, and Mrs. Davenport invites us to tea. They have a three-storeyed house, a great deal roomier than our one suite. They have a sitting-room and a dining-room on the ground floor, and bedrooms on the second and third floors. Their house is haunted. Mrs. Davenport tells my mother that they often hear steps on the stairs, and she sometimes sees an old Chinese man on the top landing. Once in a while she sees the same man sitting on the verandah. There is a stain on the floor that she can't get rid of. Every time the coolie washes it out it returns. The coolie says a murder was committed on the verandah and that the stain is blood. May takes me up to the third floor where she has her bedroom. It's a large room with a big storage cupboard. We play with our dolls until Mrs. Davenport calls May to come down for some cookies. May runs down and I'm left alone in the strange room with the ghostly murderer. It is winter and the sun sets early. The room has become dim. May has not switched on the light. May is downstairs for a long time, and I become rigid with fear. I crawl into the cupboard and pull the door shut. When May comes back she laughs at me. May is not afraid of the ghost. I can't understand it.

One day everyone is very upset. There are troubles in the city. We are all sent home from school. At home Mother is anxious about my father. The people who live upstairs drop in and tell us that there are rumours of shooting and killing, that tramcars are being overturned and that there are soldiers with machine-guns everywhere. They tell my mother that Chiang Kai-shek is routing the communists out of the city. It is 1927.

My mother looks very pale but there is nothing we can do except sit and wait and worry. I talk to my dolls about it, assuring them that my daddy will come home. I hug my teddy and remember how the conductor tossed him up in the train and how scared I was. I remember that we were on that scary train because of communists. I ask Mother what communists are. She tells me that they are people who want to help the poor by taking money away from the rich. This makes a lot of trouble and people get hurt, or even killed. She says they are the same as the Bolsheviks who forced us out of Russia by starting the revolution. I wonder if it's so bad to want to help the poor. But I suppose it's not so good when people get killed. I hope and hope that my father comes home safely. I hope so much that my throat and my chest begin to ache.

My father does come home. He doesn't smile and there's a twitch under his right eye. The trams are not running and it was a long walk home. He's exhausted and frightened. Nobody wants another revolution. It is only four years since we left Russia.

The rioters are quelled very quickly. In a couple of days all is back to normal. I hear people say that Chiang Kai-shek did the right thing to kill off those communists. May Davenport says that there are heads of the dead communists all around the city, stuck on poles. She invites me to go and see them with her. I refuse.

May says that communists and Jews are equally bad and that her mother says I shouldn't be friendly with Louba. Since the Jews killed Jesus, she points out, it's only right for Chiang Kai-shek to kill the communists. I wonder what a communist looks like but I don't dare go to look at the heads, and anyway I know Mother would never let me. I doubt if May's mother will let her go either. Chiang Kai-shek has become a great hero. His name is mentioned everywhere, but I keep thinking of those heads.

My Aunt Lena's apartment is being torn down to be replaced by a much grander building. Nina and her parents are moving into a temporary home until they can move back into the new apartment. The house they have chosen is roomy and they invite my parents to move in with them. We would have a much larger suite than we have now and the location is better. My parents agree. The house is on the fancy side of the city. The address is 8 Love Lane.

I am very excited at the idea of living with Nina. The house is palatial, three-storeyed with an attic. There are huge verandahs on each floor and coal-heating stoves in every room. The rooms are large and high-ceilinged. Lodgers occupying the flat on the third floor will soon be leaving and we will take it over. In the meantime we will live in the attic.

This attic is like a royal suite compared to other attics I

have known. It has separate rooms. There is a corner for me again.

My aunt and uncle have the flat on the second floor. There are servants' quarters below for the cook and a boy. We are not allowed to go into the servants' quarters, nor to play with their children.

My uncle has his office and waiting-room on the ground floor. There is a stained-glass window on the first landing. I have never seen a stained-glass window before and I often run down the stairs just to look at it. There is a large garden. My uncle has bought a car. It is called a Grey. There is a garage for the car. A house for a car is something new too. My uncle buys a projector and a screen and we have home movies in the sitting-room. I see Felix the Cat and Stan Laurel and Oliver Hardy. My cousin and I sit on the floor and clap our hands in delight. My sister, dignified now at sixteen, sits with the adults. Rex, my cousin's beautiful red setter, also a new acquisition, sits on the floor with us. He thumps his tail on the floor when we laugh.

There is a housewarming party in my aunt's sitting-room. Everyone is enjoying the party except my mother. She is worried about my sister who is late from school. She sends me upstairs to our attic to fetch a smocked dress she is making to show to a guest. Smocking is very fashionable. It's getting dark on the stairs for the day is closing in. I go into the gloomy attic and reach for the dress when I suddenly hear my name spoken in a low, ghostly voice. My heart stops beating. I snatch up the dress and run out. For good measure I lock the door. The key is always in the lock for when we all leave the house.

As time passes my mother becomes frantic with worry. When my father comes home she tells him my sister has not returned from school. He says we must inform the police. He goes to the attic to change. Curiously the door is locked. Behind the door is my sister in desperate pain. She sprained her ankle playing hockey and had crept up to the attic so as not to disturb the party. Her ankle had become much worse but when she tried to get out she couldn't because I had locked her in. Her ankle is horribly swollen. Everyone is cross with me. I rub away tears. I thought it was a ghost, I say.

It is summer and very hot. We congregate on the huge verandahs to keep cool. My father says it's cooler in the house, and this is true, but my cousin and I like to play on the verandah. My aunt goes to town and buys us English candy, toffees with black and white Scotch terriers on the tins, pale blue-and-white boxes of nougat and cans of Eagle-brand condensed milk. I like the condensed milk best. She ladles it out into two saucers and gives us one each. We sit primly on chairs like two little old ladies, and eat the condensed milk with tiny scoops of our spoons to make it last longer. Rex lies at our feet, panting. His tongue hangs out. There is a pool of saliva under his chin. My cousin gives Rex some of her condensed milk. But I can't make such a sacrifice. I'm too greedy.

All day long the sun shines strong and clear. The air is humid and we sweat profusely. My father suffers from prickly heat, a thick rash that covers most of his body. The cicadas saw away in the treetops. Downstairs the doctor conducts his clinic. The patients sit in armchairs in the entrance hall, complaining of the heat to one another in low voices. Sometimes my cousin and I play hide-and-seek in the big garden and in some mysterious rooms downstairs that are never used except to store furniture and luggage. We take dresses and hats out of the trunks, put them on and parade. We're elegant ladies. Rex runs around us barking. In the garden Rex chases us and tries to nip our heels. We hug him and mix our sweat with his saliva. My cousin cuts her hand. I always have cuts and scratches on my bare legs.

Rex falls ill. He is taken away in the Grey to the vet. My uncle comes home looking very grave. There are whispered consultations among the adults. We catch ominous words and phrases, a hint of panic. My cousin and I huddle in her bedroom over some books, but we're not interested in them. I think my cousin is crying.

Rex has rabies. He has been put to sleep by the vet. Tests have been conducted and there is no doubt. We will all have to have anti-rabies shots.

My uncle administers the serum. The shots are given us in our stomachs. The needle is very thick and it takes a long time for the serum to filter through. The treatment extends over several weeks. If we do not have the shots we may die like Rex.

I have a birthday and my parents give me a wonderful doll. She has curly golden hair and deep blue eyes that open and shut. She is dressed in pink silk. I have never seen anything like her in my life. The other dolls look drab beside her so I wash and iron all their clothes and redress them but the new doll still looks more beautiful. I whisper to the old dolls that I love them best no matter what.

There is a parade and my sister calls me to the window. It is a Chinese wedding procession. We watch as the musicians pass, and then the bride hidden in her ornate sedan-chair. My sister tells me that here in China the custom is for the parents to arrange the marriage and the bride and groom never see each other until after the wedding. My sister says she would never get married like that. I set my new doll against the window pane so that she can see the procession too. My mother calls us for tiffin and I run off. My beautiful doll tips over backwards, somersaults and falls flat on her face on the floor. Her porcelain head is smashed. There is only one side left. I keep the half-faced doll on my black wicker trunk for a long time. I wonder why I allowed her to come to such a sad end. The other dolls sit stony-faced. They have no answer.

The lodgers on the third floor move out and we move down from the attic. It's wonderful for everyone except me. I have to share my parents' bedroom. Even though it's a very large room it's not the same as having a corner of my own. We have two bedrooms, a dining-room and a kitchen. Nina shares the second bedroom with my sister and I hear them having fun at bedtime, whispering and giggling. We use the common sitting-room downstairs for special occasions.

May Davenport and her mother come to visit us. May has always loved my dolls and particularly their clothes. My mother has taken time out of her busy life to make these clothes. I show off my latest acquisitions to May Davenport. We are called into the dining-room for tea. My mother has made little sandwiches and there is a cake layered with custard. Mrs. Davenport compliments Mother on the cake and says she sometimes regrets that she has a cook as she never gets a chance to make anything herself. My mother says that that is indeed a pity and that we too have a cook downstairs but that she likes to do a bit in the kitchen herself sometimes. My mother is prettier than Mrs. Davenport, who has a long nose and frizzy hair, but I suddenly realize that my mother's English is not very good. I have not thought of this before. I wish it were better.

May and I tuck in. After tea we play and all too soon it is time for May and her mother to leave. Later I find that some of my dolls' clothes are missing. I search everywhere but I can't find them. Mother says the clothes will turn up, not to worry. The clothes do not turn up. Two or three days later Mrs. Davenport telephones my mother and apologizes, saying that May took some of my dolls' clothes home by mistake among her own things. My mother accepts Mrs. Davenport's excuses but she has a funny look on her face when she returns from the phone. Some time later she shows me a dress and bonnet she has made. They are for May Davenport's doll. She says if May has something nice of her own she won't take other people's things.

There is a contest in the children's section of the North China Daily News, the main Shanghai newspaper. The contest asks for stories from children between eight and ten. My sister says I should enter the contest. I am dismayed, but I'm used to obeying her so I write a story, laboriously, and mail it to the paper. One day my name is published as the winner of the contest. My sister and I take a trip down to the North China Daily News office and a smiling gentleman shakes my hand and gives me a splendid edition of *Alice's Adventures in Wonderland.* I can't believe it. I have never had such a fine book. I carry it home in the tramcar with great care. At home everyone admires my prize.

Mrs. Davenport phones Mother and tells her I won the prize unfairly. May also sent in a story but did not win anything. She says it is perfectly clear to her that my sister helped me write the story. My mother rejects the accusation. Her English is more stumbly than ever. The next day I find that one of my dolls is wearing the dress Mother made for May Davenport's doll. In school May Davenport doesn't talk to me. It is my first encounter with the dark side of success.

Many people come to visit my Aunt Lena, immigrants the family has known in Vladivostok, their relations and friends, some genuinely friendly, others, so my elders whisper, hoping to get an in with the doctor, or perhaps with a family rapidly becoming well-to-do. Among these is a slick young man called Fedya Unjenin. I don't like him very much. My Aunt Lena and my mother giggle a bit when they talk about him. Fedya is tall, slim and blond. I do not know it, but he is a lady's man. One evening Fedya is invited to dinner. There is a flutter among the women folk. It makes me wary and uncomfortable. When the grownups go down to Aunt Lena's sitting-room to greet and entertain the visitor, I look at myself in the mirror of my mother's dresser. I look at myself critically. I pick up a jar of my father's brilliantine and plaster down my fly-away hair. My head now looks smooth and round. I go down.

I am greeted with cries of dismay. "Whatever have you done to your hair?" a family member cries.

"What's all that greasy stuff you've put on it?" another

wants to know.

"You look like a football," a third declares.

"Oh hush," says a lady friend, who is about to turn my heart into a ball of fury, "can't you see? She's done it for Fedya. She's beautified herself for Fedya. Why, Fedya, she's in love with you!"

The whole room bursts out laughing. I stand, colouring to the roots of my sticky, plastered-down hair, hating the whole lot of them. "No, I'm not!" I shout. "I'm not, I'm not!"

Fedya comes across the room and puts an arm around me, but I break away from him and flee from the room of cruel, laughing adults.

I run back up the stairs and throw myself on my bed in a torrent of tears. I am so mortified I wish myself dead.

But I have learned something. I have learned what it is to be betrayed. I place betrayal at the very top of my list of crimes. It will always stay there.

Someone gives my sister six ducklings. They all die except one. We call him Jinky and he lives in a box in our bathroom. He swims in the bath. The bath stands on claw feet. We put a board in the bath and he climbs up on it and dives off. Every time he dives, Kewpie, our newly acquired pet, a fox terrier, darts under the bath. We spend hours at this sport.

Some of our possessions have gone missing. My aunt questions the house boy. He tells her that they have been stolen by a ghost. He says there are three kinds of ghosts, ghosts who make noises, ghosts who smell and ghosts who steal. A few nights later my doctor uncle catches the house boy on the verandah with one of his suits. The police are called and the ghost is laid.

The house is plunged into gloom. My sister has become ill. She is very ill indeed. My doctor uncle climbs the stairs several times a day with his slow, heavy steps and examines her. He stands beside her bed with his hands steepled, raised to his chin, contemplating. My sister has typhoid fever. Her dishes have to be sterilized. My cousin and I are not allowed into her room. She is ill for a long time. The whole house is hushed. My Aunt Lena takes me to school, now a long way away since we have come to live at 8 Love Lane in the fancy part of town, and picks me up at four in the afternoon. This allows my mother to nurse my sister. At last my sister starts to mend. My mother starts to smile again. My father hugs us both, tells us how glad he is, how much he loves us. He is so happy it is sadder than when he was anxious.

My sister's head has been shaved. She is glad, she hopes her hair will grow in curly. It doesn't but I don't think it matters. She's ever so pretty anyhow.

Chapter Five

Yesterday at my home in Vancouver, in the egalitarian eighties, I had some friends in to dinner. My cousin came in a new dress marvellously rich in colour, a petunia red, with mauve undertones. It suited her well and I exclaimed over it. She was having one of her "good" days and she looked handsome and pleased and animated.

She preceded me into the living-room walking carefully, leaning on her cane. I followed with my Aunt Lena, my arm around her shoulders. Her bones are like a bird's. If you have ever held the fragile body of a bird in your hand you will know how my aunt's bones feel under my fingers. My aunt said: "I hate red." As always she spoke in Russian. As near as translation serves, our colloquy proceeded something like this:

"What red?" I asked, in Russian too.

"Any red. That red. Nina's dress."

"How can you say that?" I cried. "It's a gorgeous dress."

"I hate red," my aunt repeated, with an impatient little shrug.

"But why?" I asked, stupidly.

"Because the Reds took Russia away from me," said my aunt simply. "I hate everything red."

After a moment I said, "Well, Nina's dress isn't really *red*. It has a lot of mauve in it. It's really raspberry."

"It's red," my aunt said. "Krasnaya, krasnaya."

I slipped my hand down her arm and took hers, so dry, so veined. I led her into the living-room to introduce her to those of my friends she didn't know. And, holding her dry, veined hand, I was instantly transported to another time, another place, transported so vividly that I was struck with vertigo. I left her in the care of my friends and went back to the kitchen to be by myself for a little while.

Another place, another time. My aunt and I are walking down a hot, dusty street. My head reaches only to her shoulder. She holds my hand tightly as if afraid that in some magic way I shall suddenly vanish. I am not, after all, her child, and she feels her responsibility deeply. This is one of those days when she is taking me home from school. Ever since my sister's illness she has been picking me up after school once in a while to give my mother a little break. My mother and Aunt Lena don't think I'm old enough to go all that way by myself.

We walk past a Japanese cobbler's and I wrinkle my nose. There's a pungent smell of sour cabbage. My aunt shakes her head at me. It's rude to show your feelings if they are not favourable. We come to the Sikh quarter and I can smell what I know is their cooking oil, but it is alien to me, and strong, so I break from my aunt's hold and race to the end of the block. She lets me go, following at a gracious pace. When she rejoins me she says that we're just not used to it. She recaptures my hand and admits that it *is* strong but that we must never offend people. I could hold my breath, she suggests.

My aunt, who has never said a rude word to anyone in her whole life, now smiles at me. She tells me that she understands my feelings but that our cooking must smell as strange to them as theirs does to us. She always says this but I always run just the same.

Further on we pass a Greek store. Here we stop and enter. It is dark and smells of coffee. My aunt makes purchases while I prowl around the store. It is a deep store, its walls lined with tubs full of strange grains and nuts and dried fruit and brittle macaroni. There are tubs of olives floating in their juices. I bend over these and inhale. My nose just tips the slightly scummy liquid. My aunt sees me and rebukes me gently. She rolls her large eyes and shakes her head. I am abashed.

We pass a Russian bakery. We go in here too and buy a dozen boobliki. These are like bagels with the hole in the centre, but they are lighter and crunchy and covered with sesame seeds. I can't wait to eat them. The fragrance of the fresh bread torments me but I know I must suffer till we get home. My hands are dirty and eating on the street is simply not done. Only Chinese and beggars eat on the street.

We wait for a tramcar on the corner of Soochow Road and Broadway, just across from the Garden Bridge that spans the Soochow Creek at the point where it joins the Whangpoo River. Here they have started work on the foundations for a very large building. It is going to be called The Broadway Mansions. But before construction can start they have to pump out huge quantities of water and drive in massive piles. I watch the coolies hard at work. There seems to be no end to the water they have to pump out. My aunt says that the whole of Shanghai is built on a swamp. She must be right, though the pavement under my feet seems solid enough.

Our tramcar arrives and we board. We go into the first-class compartment. There is a second-class in our car and a third-class in a completely separate car trailing behind. This third-class car has no seats and is very cheap. It is so tightly packed that there are people hanging out of the door as the tramcar wends its way down the street, clanging its bell. I'm always afraid that someone will fall out and that there will be a dreadful accident. There never is.

The tramcars, even the first-class compartments, are grubby and the floors are littered. Today two Japanese ladies sit opposite us. They look like the dolls my sister gave me. Their faces are made up with very thick white powder, almost like a paste, and their eyes and brows are heavily outlined. Their lips are scarlet. Their black coiffures are huge and perfectly rigid. If the roof of the tramcar caves in these ladies will be quite squashed, but their coiffures will remain intact.

My aunt sits looking out of the window, holding her groceries in her lap with one hand. With the other she still clutches mine as if I might suddenly vanish, through the seat of the car perhaps. I look up at her. A fashionable hat sits atop her thick, wavy, dark hair. She is handsome rather than pretty. She has fine eyes, but her nose is a shade too severe. This nose, and the set of her lips, make her look determined. And she *is* determined. A tiny woman of phenomenal strength of mind, acumen and integrity. At this age I am unable to verbalize these qualities, I only admire her and have total faith in her without knowing why.

The tramcar stops periodically. I look out at the street outside, teeming with Chinese people. I see rickshaws and bicycles, waggons and wheelbarrows. On one wheelbarrow four young girls are taking a joy-ride, laughing and shouting. A country woman, clutching a basket of clucking panic-stricken chickens, dodges between the vehicles. From my safe seat on the tramcar I see cars moving slowly through, tooting their horns almost constantly. The city folk are skilful at ignoring rules of traffic. They crowd, push, dart, and are not caught. But bewildered newcomers from the country get a taste of the Sikh policemen's truncheons.

I have been watching a cyclist out of the window. He rides alongside the tram, zigzagging skilfully through the traffic, is left behind as the tram forges ahead and catches up when the tram stops. It's like a race and I watch for him eagerly at each stop. Then, at one point when he's ahead of us and the tram's rattling to overtake him again, a car comes up behind him loudly and arrogantly tooting its way through the traffic. For a moment the cyclist is caught between the car and the tram, then he loses his balance and falls. He pitches forward and his cycle crashes in the path of the tram.

The tram driver applies his brakes with a great noise of squealing and grinding and so suddenly that everyone in the compartment is thrown forward. My aunt loses her hold on her bag of groceries, the bag falls and to my dismay six of the precious boobliki roll out in every direction all over the filthy floor.

"Oh my God!" cries my aunt, her composure shattered for a terrible moment. She picks up the grocery bag gingerly and sets it on the seat, holding it in her gloved hands a little away from her clothes and looking distastefully at the side that has been in contact with the floor. The fallen boobliki of course have to be abandoned. Three are lying quite close to us and these my aunt kicks under the seat.

Outside a loud hubbub has arisen. The tram driver, the cyclist and the chauffeur of the car are shouting at one another and a huge crowd has gathered. The cyclist is rubbing his neck and shoulder. His cycle was tossed aside by the curved steel cage at the front of the tramcar but it is sadly damaged. A fat lady in a fancy hat inside the car is gesticulating through the open window. I see a large policeman bearing down upon the group. After a few moments of conversation between the policeman and the chauffeur I see money passing between the policeman and the woman, and the policeman then starts to berate the unfortunate cyclist. The cyclist protests, the tram driver, certainly innocent, protests, but the large policeman clouts the cyclist on the head and the driver on his back with his truncheon and sends them both about their business. The driver returns to the tram, the cyclist picks up his cycle and retires to the sidewalk to nurse his wounds and the lady is driven off in the grand car. I seethe at the injustice I have witnessed. I grieve for the lost boobliki.

We finally arrive home with our groceries and the remains of our boobliki and our frightful tale of the accident. But before we can begin telling it we are engulfed by far greater news, news that totally eclipses our story. A letter has arrived informing my doctor uncle that the apartment they are waiting for has been finished and is ready for occupancy. Moreover we hear that the house we are all living in, our 8 Love Lane, has been sold by its owner. We too will have to find another home. Total upheaval faces us.

My mother and father start house-hunting the very next day. There is a new complex of terrace houses going up in one of the better sections of the city, on Bubbling Well Road, not too far from my aunt's new home-to-be. The name of this complex is Sun Avenue. It will be shortly ready for occupancy. My parents decide to rent in Sun Avenue. They take me to see the almost completed homes.

I fall in love with Sun Avenue. The houses are painted a bright yellow. They are two-storeyed, not large and with only tiny yards, but what delights me about them is that they have three bedrooms. This means that I will have my very own room. A whole room! I will not have to share it with anyone.

My ecstasy is somewhat dampened by the fact that we have to give Jinky away. We can't keep a duck in the terrace house, nor can my aunt keep him in her apartment. She approaches friends who have a large house and garden much like the one we are leaving at 8 Love Lane. They also have a pond in the backyard. These people agree to take Jinky and to my great sorrow we deliver him to their home. Months later we are invited to dine with these people. We are served something that isn't chicken. I ask whatever happened to Jinky? After a few moments of stunned silence my mother says, "Don't be silly, dear."

The house on Sun Avenue is bright and clean and smells of fresh paint. My wicker trunk is moved in and I sit my dolls on it in three rows. I have a large desk against one wall, bought at another auction, on which I arrange my textbooks, my pencil case and ruler and my brand new shiny geometry set. There are some scratches on the desk which bother me, but I cover them with a large blotting-paper pad. My inkpot and its pen sit at the top righthand corner of the pad. I have won more prizes in the newspaper competitions, all books, and I display these proudly on my new (to me) desk.

I still sleep in my old crib although I am ten years old. My feet now push up against the netting, but I'm a very small ten and the crib is large. I still fit in. My sister utters dire warnings. She says I shall never grow if I sleep in such a small bed. She quotes the example of the goldfish in a small bowl and those in large ponds that grow to be carp. I don't like being compared to a goldfish. She says I'll go bald if I keep rubbing my head up against the netting. I am distressed. My mother scolds. There have been many expenses connected with the move and a new bed is out of the question while the old one is still functional. I am promised that a new bed will have top priority in future spending.

I am reconciled to my stunted growth and my balding head when I contemplate the other wonders of this room of my very own. In the corner by the window I have a small rattan table my mother bought for me at the Chinese basket fair. The basket fair comes to Shanghai every year and spreads over several blocks of Bubbling Well Road displaying every imaginable kind of rattan, bamboo and woven ware. I have covered my rattan table with an embroidered cloth and placed upon it a Bible I have won as a prize at Sunday School for knowing all the year's texts by heart. Sending me to Sunday School was my sister's idea. She had been indoctrinated into the Anglican Church at school. She attends church regularly and takes me with her. I sit through tedious mornings of readings and hymns and an endless sermon every Sunday, and then at three o'clock I go to the Sunday School. My sister takes me there and picks me up. She is very conscientious about it. My parents are lukewarm religionists. The only Lutheran church in Shanghai is the German church and although my father is fluent in German my mother does not understand it. Also Sunday is my father's only day of rest, so churchgoing is not on my parents' weekend itinerary.

Sunday School is excruciatingly boring but I go because my sister says it's good for me. We are given a text to memorize every week. I have discovered that I can memorize everything I read. It's a wonderful way to pass exams. I do not make any great effort to understand what I memorize, or to relate one piece of knowledge to another. I simply memorize. My memory is prodigious but I don't know that so I think everyone memorizes like I do. Verses, texts, dates, whole pages of prose stick to my brain like glue. Sometimes I try to shake them off when they run so endlessly through my head, like an internalized ticker-tape, but I never get rid of them. So I have memorized a whole year of texts with no effort, run them off in an oral test and received a Bible. It has coloured pictures of Jesus and the great prophets and a handsome cover. Beside the Bible on my rattan table, I place a blue triangular-shaped glass vase my father has given me for my birthday and try to keep it always full of flowers. My sister says I will knock the vase over and ruin the prize Bible. I ignore her warning.

In our Sun Avenue home we have a marvellous new feature, a flush toilet. Even the palatial 8 Love Lane did not have such a luxury. No more "modoong" amahs. There is a tank high up on the wall with a long chain. When you pull the chain everything swirls for a moment and then vanishes. It's magic.

We acquire a gramophone. It's a square box of highly polished brown wood with a cover that opens up and clicks into place to reveal a turntable and an arm. At the side of the box there is a handle that has to be wound to keep the turntable spinning. There is also a small container for tiny wooden needles. The gramophone stands on a table and has become the focal point of our sitting-room. We have a number of records, popular songs and light operas. A man singing in a passionate voice tells me that he is the sheikh of Araby and that my love belongs to him. I think of Vickery. He tells me that at night when I'm asleep he'll to my window creep. It's very exciting and I forget to wind the turntable so that the record slows and the romantic sheikh's voice deteriorates to an undistinguishable drone. Everyone in the room shouts at me. For some reason winding up the gramophone is my duty. My sister chooses the pieces and carefully lowers the arm. My father sharpens the wooden needles with his penknife after every three or four records. Mother sits on the sofa, hands folded, head resting on the sofa back, eyes closed, smiling faintly.

In Sun Avenue I fall in love again. The object of my affections is called Sonnyboy and lives a few houses away from us. I see him passing our house, whistling, very cavalier. He has blond curly hair and is thirteen years old. I love him passionately. I'm sure he loves me. I try to whistle like he does but my mother tells me that whistling is only for boys and reminds me of the old Russian superstition that says if you whistle in the house you'll whistle away all your money.

It is winter. Magically snow falls. We have very cold winters, with winds blowing straight from Mongolia, but it seldom snows. I am delighted with the snow. I and the little servant girl, our amah, go out into the tiny front yard and build a snowman. Sonnyboy comes by and offers a carrot for a nose and two pieces of coal for eyes. I love him more than ever.

Sonnyboy shows me a beebee gun he has been given for his birthday. He aims it at a little sparrow sitting on the fence. He fires the gun and the sparrow falls. I scream and run to the sparrow. Sonnyboy is delighted with his skill. I touch the sparrow gingerly. His little body is quite limp, his eyes half shut. I fall out of love.

I catch cold and cough a lot. My mother melts sugar in a ladle over a gas flame, stirring it with a silver spoon, pours in a measure of vodka and lights it. When the flame dies down there is a delicious candy on the spoon and a thick syrup in the ladle. The cough disappears. I wish I could get another.

It is spring. We go out to dinner to my aunt's house and there is a great thunderstorm. Lightning flashes, the thunder roars and rain comes down in straight grey sheets. In no time at all the city is awash. We wait out the storm and return home in the late evening through streets washed clean, a bonanza of the storm. We do not have to pick our way between gobs of spittle. The air is heady with spring perfumes. At home I find I have left my window open and the wind has overturned the blue vase on my rattan table. It has fallen on my Bible and the water has soaked through the cover. Even my name on the pasted-in certificate is smudged. My little shrine has been destroyed. I begin to brood on the cruelties of life and nature, and the fragility of sacredness, and I start to worry again about my stunted growth and my balding head.

To add to my miseries we have a visitation of bedbugs. Suddenly our beds come alive with small, fat, red creepy-crawlies. I wake in the morning covered with itchy spots. My parents speculate on the origin of the bugs. They must have come in with the clean sheets from the Chinese laundry. Two are enough, my mother says mysteriously. My father says that they are practically indestructible, that bedbugs found in tombs of the pharoahs have been known to revive after a good meal and start to breed again. I am filled with bone-deep horror. I can see the bedbugs multiplying to fill my room, the house, the yard. Indestructible. I know what the bedbugs consider a good meal. My skin crawls. I scratch and scratch.

My mother and the amah take the beds apart and place the hollow metal tubing in the bath. Then they pour boiling water down the tubes. I watch as hundreds of bedbugs are washed out of the tubes and down the drains. The amah hauls the bed frames outside and pours boiling water into every corner and crevice. More bedbugs are washed away. Even though I am glad to be rid of them I am appalled at how quickly and ruthlessly they have been destroyed.

My sister falls in love. They have met in an elevator. He is from New Zealand and is studying to become a health inspector. He has a defect, his left hand is missing. She is going to bring him home to meet Mother and Father. His name is Jack.

I meet my sister's friend. He is the handsomest young man I have ever seen. He wears an artificial left hand with a white glove on it. I have been warned not to say anything about it but I am curious and have difficulty in keeping my eyes away from his hand. My parents think he is a nice enough young man but are very anxious about the hand. Is it a hereditary trait? my father asks my doctor uncle the next time he sees him. It doesn't have to be, my doctor uncle hedges. My father is not reassured.

Worse follows. My sister's friend develops a cough. It is discovered that he has tuberculosis. This is serious news indeed. I see blood on his handkerchief when he coughs into it. My sister's friend has to leave town to live in a sanatorium in the mountains. Life in our bright Sun Avenue home darkens. For comfort I open my damaged Bible, a symbol now of the fragility of earthly happiness. The blurred name on the pasted-in certificate only serves to depress me further. What does it mean, one's name? So easily blurred, so easily washed out.

My sister and I both write letters to her friend in the sanatorium. He writes back and we hear that he is improving. My sister looks hopeful but my parents are still gloomy—tuberculosis has a way of recurring, you never know whether you're rid of it or not. It is contagious and often fatal. People die from it all the time.

But my sister's friend does not die. He continues to improve and one day we hear that he is coming home. Life loses its fragility, becomes everlasting again.

Chapter Six

On Sun Avenue Maria Mikhailovna enters our life. Her entry is preceded by a period of mystery. I begin to hear snippets of conversation, vaguely ominous remarks, veiled allusions, all to do with my Uncle Ernest. I don't know my Uncle Ernest very well and connect him only with the traumatic episode of the exploding gas heater in the house where we lived with my Aunt Lena. He did not figure in the life we led on the northeast side of the city, nor did he appear at 8 Love Lane. In the excitement of school and new friends and experiences he has receded to the background of my mind.

From the vaguely ominous remarks and the veiled allusions, I soon gather that Uncle Ernest has incurred the deep disapproval of my Aunt Lena. I learn that he has married a woman nine years his senior without regard for Aunt Lena's opinion. Murkily I understand that a rift has taken place.

The rift is deeply wounding to everyone. Uncle Ernest is so much younger than my mother and Aunt Lena that they look upon him more as a son than a brother. They feel they have been instrumental in bringing him up and so are indirectly responsible for his actions. He feels a loyalty to them as he would to his mother who is now far away in Vladivostok. But he is in love.

I don't know very much about the mores of the times, but I understand that they are ranged against the lovers. It appears that Uncle Ernest has done something very wrong. By keeping my ears open I learn further that not only is the woman older than Uncle Ernest but she is also a divorcée. I have never heard of divorce before. Divorce between my parents would be utterly inconceivable. Such a possibility never even occurs to me. The woman Uncle Ernest has married presents herself to my mind as someone unnatural, a monster of sorts. The matter is scandalous. From time to time I hear the woman's name mentioned, Maria Mikhailovna. This is the Russian formal mode of address—a combination of the first name and a patronym.

I now find that my Uncle Ernest is often at our house when I come home from school. He and my mother have long conversations while I'm doing my homework or playing. They make no attempt to keep these conversations private, there is no lowering of voices. They don't consider me of sufficient importance, nor do they imagine that anything they say can be of concern to me. It's not my business. But I'm curious. Although all is by no means clear I begin to understand that Uncle Ernest is asking my mother to act as a mediator between him and my Aunt Lena. He is extremely distressed by the rift that has taken place. He tells my mother that he can't live without Maria Mikhailovna, that my mother must persuade my Aunt Lena to see it his way.

My mother is judgmental. She herself does not approve of what Uncle Ernest has done. She feels divorce is a major crime. She tells Uncle Ernest that he has made a great mistake, that he will suffer for it. Rather coldly, she tells him that Aunt Lena is right.

My Uncle Ernest is slim, not tall, charmingly fresh-faced. His hair stands up in fascinating blond waves all over his head. He is persuasive. He tells my mother that the rift is devastating to him. He reminds her of the importance of family unity, of the damaging effects of a family feud. She retorts that he should have thought of that before. He dredges up the deepest fear of all socially oriented persons—he points out that a family feud will *fuel gossip.* It will be malicious, pleased gossip, he says. People will be delighted that there is trouble in our family.

My mother agrees to act as mediator. When we go to visit Aunt Lena I hear the same subject raised again and again. I hear it said that Maria Mikhailovna is an infamous, scheming woman. She has bewitched my Uncle Ernest. Against this is weighed the threat of the likely gossip. I am totally ignored in these consultations but my interest is snowballing. I'm dying to meet this extraordinary woman. I wonder what she is like. I picture someone very beautiful of course, romantic, but evil, like one of the bad fairies in my storybooks.

My mother and Aunt Lena reach a compromise. My mother will receive Maria Mikhailovna first. She will assess her. Then, based on my mother's assessment, my aunt might perhaps relent. My mother has been a successful emissary. Or has the thought of what people will say about the break in our family facilitated an attempt at reconciliation? We have never had any familial disagreements and people resent our complacence.

One day I hear that Uncle Ernest and Maria Mikhailovna are coming to visit. The thought of meeting a divorcée engrosses me. I make an unprecedented error in my math homework.

They arrive at our house in a Peugeot. It is a small green car and they come, ostensibly, to take my mother and me to the Hongkew Market. I have spent the morning looking out of the window so as not to miss their arrival, and at last they are here. But the controversial Maria Mikhailovna, getting out of the green Peugeot, is nothing like what I expected. She does not in the least resemble a wicked fairy posing as a sweetly romantic beauty. The woman I see is plump, with pleasant but unremarkable features and thick, reddish-brown hair arranged in fashionable marcel waves and shingled at the back. She looks like another aunt to me. Fleetingly I wonder why my Uncle Ernest was willing to quarrel with someone like my Aunt Lena for the sake of this woman.

I stand rather shyly in the doorway. I am introduced and I curtsy—I am not yet old enough to discard this charming custom. Maria Mikhailovna puts her hands on my shoulders and looks down at me with warm brown eyes. I am still small at eleven. Then she puts her arms around me and gives me a close hug. Her bosom is large and soft and my head sinks into it. I am engulfed in a delicious perfume. She gives me a gift.

It is a baby doll, about six inches long, which she has dressed entirely in wool. She is a talented knitter and the clothes are exquisite, like lace. There is a crib for the doll, padded and trimmed with satin and ribbons and complete with a tiny mattress and bedclothes.

Never have I been so enchanted with a gift.

I can't believe my luck. The unkind whispers I have heard about Maria Mikhailovna seem to me unjustified and unfair. I can't see the scheming trouble-maker I have been led to expect in this winning person.

We drive to the Hongkew Market. This is the best market in the city located in the northeast end and not far from my school. Lately I have begun to notice how inferior the northeast side of the city is compared to our present surroundings, but the Hongkew Market is still full of wonders. In spite of the floors, which are always wet and slimy, and sometimes, by the beef and chicken stalls, bloody, in spite of the crush and the noise and the huge draughts that billow perpetually through the open-ended premises benumbing us in winter, the Hongkew Market is the most exciting place in my world.

There are stalls laden with vegetables and fruit and farm produce of every kind. There are crates of live chickens, squawking in indignation, tanks of fish, crabs squirming on long strings, rows of Peking ducks, red and shiny, formidable sides of beef and pork, hot noodles and deep-fried dough-balls, baked sweet potatoes, and, in the fall, the marvellous aroma of roasting chestnuts. Stands overflow with flowers, tuck counters peddle hot red ginger and sweet, sticky mango stones, and household marvels, chatties, bamboo and metal ware and astonishing straw hats jostle for attention. A magnificent selection, but today we are going primarily to buy a specially prepared Japanese fish.

This fish is the most delicious food of its kind I have ever tasted. It is sweet and sour and juicy and when we bring it home Mother will crisp it in her pan. She used to bring it home as a treat when we lived on the east side, but the Hongkew Market is far away now so she seldom goes there. Today distance is of no consequence because we have come to the market with Uncle Ernest and Maria Mikhailovna in their car.

I cuddle my new doll and slop around between the stalls of produce. Maria Mikhailovna says she will buy me whatever I want. My mother is dismayed and warns her that she could end up buying the whole market. Why not? asks Maria Mikhailovna, for such a darling little girl. I am enchanted by some tiny paper umbrellas. I ask for one. Maria Mikhailovna buys me half a dozen. We go home laden with purchases and at home we fry and eat the wonderful sweet and sour Japanese fish.

Now that I have met Maria Mikhailovna I listen more carefully than ever when I hear her name mentioned. I gather that Maria Mikhailovna is part heiress to a fortune. It appears that this fortune means little to her, and she has persuaded Uncle Ernest to throw up his job and live a life of pleasure and mild dissipation. This alarms even my easy-going mother, and of course my Aunt Lena, who is generous but thrifty, is appalled.

However relations have been established with my mother and there are more visits and more gifts. In time I hear that Aunt Lena has relented and that Uncle Ernest and Maria Mikhailovna will be received in her house. This pleases me enormously.

We are now seeing a great deal of Uncle Ernest and Maria Mikhailovna. She introduces us to her twin sister, Anna Mikhailovna, her husband and five children. Uncle Ernest laughs, jokes, teases. He portrays the carefree side of life as opposed to my doctor uncle's less charismatic, if more dependable, gravity. And one day he opens a window for me on a totally novel and delightful prospect—he takes us for a ride in the green Peugeot into the countryside around Shanghai.

I have never been out of the city since we arrived from Vladivostok. I give little thought to its location. I know we are close to a great river, but the fact that a vast country lies to the west and extends north and south of us hardly enters my perception at all. Now, with Uncle Ernest and Maria Mikhailovna we drive out of the city. We leave behind us the streets and houses and the milling crowds and we enter a different world. The green Peugeot chugs along dirt roads, past clusters of curious black-roofed houses, by stagnant, moss-covered creeks and between fields extending on every side to the curve of the earth. I see men and women dressed in faded blue, wearing conical hats, working close to the soil or pushing squeaky wheelbarrows between undeviating rows of crops. I see water buffaloes for the first time and Uncle Ernest explains the mysteries of the waterwheel to me. I see burial mounds. But most of all I am impressed with the sense of endless space. The city shrinks behind me. I breathe in great draughts of air. The horizons spin around me.

Awareness explodes in my head. There is a big world outside.

This vision is not threatening. Big world it may be, but I'm still its centre. My experience has only added a new and exciting dimension to my secure home life. It even seems cosier and safer by comparison. I am a very contented child at this time.

My east end school is a Spartan one but we children are unaware of this. We think all schools are like ours. The building is old, the floors are stained and splintery and the uneven steps of the staircases creak ominously. It is a magnificent firetrap. At one side of the school a courtyard, only partially protected from the weather, accommodates a row of toilets, and a long cement sink fitted with only cold-water taps. Here we perform our ablutions before lunch. In the winter basins are placed along the length of the sink into which a Chinese servant pours boiling water. Cold water is added from the taps and we take turns to wash our hands. If we happen to be at the end of the line we are faced with a dark-grey soup topped with a layer of pure filth. The more finicky among us then wash our hands in the freezing water from the taps. At this time of the year my hands are always chapped and bleeding, and Mother treats them overnight with a breath-stopping solution of glycerine, alcohol and eau de cologne. Miraculously the lesions are always healed by morning.

From the upstairs windows of the school, we have a view of the compound next door that encloses a church and monastic quarters, and the girls giggle peeking at the serious monks who parade below, and are punished if they are caught at this perfidious occupation. I am fascinated by the monks and wonder how they can live like that, always secluded in that dreary compound. They walk with prayer books in their hands. Our teacher tells us that their lives have been given to God and it is wicked to giggle at them. I wonder what it means to give your life to God.

We play catch and tag, hopscotch and rope games on the cement playing-grounds, there is no grass anywhere, and we become used to bloodied knees and gravelly palms. The classrooms are never warm enough in winter and unbearably hot in summer but we take all these things in our stride, and at the end of the day I can return to my lovely bright-yellow Sun Avenue home. All kinds of delicious smells always emanate from the kitchen, and when I run upstairs, there are my dolls, my tidy desk with its books, my table in the corner with the damaged but still beloved Bible and the triangular blue vase of flowers. My very own room. And there is my mother engaged in her own mysterious pursuits, the personification of security.

When I first started school I was shy. Small and unimpressive, I suffered torments when I wasn't chosen in classroom games like "The Farmer's in the Dell" or "I Sent a Letter to my Lover." I sweated with anxiety as girl after girl passed me by and no-one left the magic letter behind my back or when I wasn't chosen even for the "cheese." But I have grown inured to this. I'm patient and I wait, hoping that something will happen to make me more noteworthy in the eyes of my peers.

At the prize-giving ceremony every year, each class stages a presentation. Our class is to dramatize the trials and final triumph of Perseus in acquiring the head of the Medusa. I am not chosen for any of the main roles and my disappointment is almost unbearable. I am to be, with the majority of the class, only a guest at the banquet, the scene where Perseus appears with the head of the Medusa, tears off her shroud and holds the grisly trophy aloft, turning the wicked king and his court to stone. The drama of that moment curdles my brain. I would give anything to be Perseus. But it is not to be. A taller, more impressive child has been chosen.

And then, on the morning of the great day, the tall impressive child is reported ill. There is no Perseus, and so there will be no contribution from our form to the ceremonies. I am not a bold child but I recognize that something truly important is at stake. I put my terrors aside and approach the teacher, whose mood is not of the best. She has worked hard on our presentation.

I swallow hard. "Please, Miss Ferguson," I say, "I could do Perseus."

She stares at me as if I've lost my senses. We had no understudies, she tells me testily, how can I know the part? Her voice shakes. She sounds very annoyed. She is regretting this obviously foolish omission on her part. Everyone knows children exasperatingly come down with mumps and measles at the most inappropriate moments.

"I do know it," I insist, shaking in every limb. "I know the whole play by heart."

She glowers at me. But she is no fool. She has always suspected me of having a trick memory. She agrees to let me try out, though she's still doubtful.

But of course I do know the whole play by heart. I haven't spent a minute memorizing it. It seeped through my skull as I watched rehearsals and remained hopelessly glued to my flypaper brain.

I get the part of Perseus. We put on our show. I am a heroine. We even get the award for the best presentation. And to top my joy I also receive a General Progress prize, an elegantly bound edition of *The Arabian Nights Entertainments.* Louba congratulates me, pleased with her protégée.

Back at home I recount my doings and am hugged and kissed and made much of. My dolls witness over and over again the enactment of the play in my room where I take all the parts and where they are the courtiers of the wicked king and have the distinction of being turned to stone again and again by the fearful head of the Medusa. I cannot be happier.

And then my whole life is overturned.

Chapter Seven

The door is shut. My parents are having a long discussion in their bedroom. I am curious and a little anxious—they very seldom shut their door. It's Sunday and my sister has just brought me home from Sunday School. I ask her what my parents are talking about and she says we'll know soon. I offer to fix up her room and she agrees. I often do this because I love to arrange things and she's too busy leading her interesting late-teen life to bother. She goes off downstairs to listen to her radio. As I put away her clothes neatly, set out the combs and brushes, and dust the jars and bottles on her dresser, I hear the murmur of conversation from my parents' bedroom. My anxiety grows. At last my mother comes out. She smiles at me and looks much as usual. She has gradually been changing her hairstyle and has recently had her hair marcel-waved. She now wears it close to her head. She nods when I show her what I've done in my sister's room and then she goes down to give orders to the amah to make some tea and to get dinner under way. I am mystified.

We sit down to tea at the dining-room table and have little half-moon almond cookies, which my mother makes by pressing out the dough with the rim of a wineglass. My mother says, "We're going to move house."

She might have dropped a bomb on my plate.

My sister doesn't seem surprised. She must have known all along what the conversation had been about. Only I had been kept out of it. But that is not unusual. Nobody pays any attention to me when something important is being discussed.

The cookies on the table lose their appeal. I don't feel hungry any more. I can't believe what I just heard. I thought I'd live in Sun Avenue to the end of my life.

"Where are we going?" I ask.

My mother explains that Uncle Ernest and Maria Mikhailovna are looking for more economical accommodation and a new complex of terrace houses has just been completed on a street called Avenue Haig. This street is on the border between the International Settlement and the French Concession and it is not too far from our Bubbling Well Road. The houses are larger than our Sun Avenue home and we will be sharing one of these houses with Uncle Ernest and Maria Mikhailovna. We will be living in a better house but at the same time it will be more economical for us too. Mother will be able to afford more help, a manservant instead of only a little amah, and perhaps a manservant with a wife. It will make things much easier for her. And what is more, and of greater importance, says my mother, suddenly zeroing in on me, our improved financial position will also allow me to go to another school.

"Another school!" I echo.

My mother tells me that this is Nina's school. It will be so close to our new home that I'll be able to walk there. It's a much better school. She and I are going to see the new house the very next day. The complex is called Victory Terrace.

I run out of the room up to my bedroom and curl up on my old crib in despair. I tell my dolls about the terrible things that are going to happen. For the first time in my life I suddenly know I'm too old to be talking to my dolls.

After a while my sister comes up and comforts me. I'll like the new school, she says. It *is* a better school and a good student like me should get the best education possible. She tells me I'll learn to play tennis there.

But my heart is broken. I can't believe any house can be as nice as our Sun Avenue home.. I don't care about the new school and the educational opportunities. I can't bear the thought of leaving all my friends. I've just started to make my mark among them. I'm almost popular. I don't care about tennis. I just want things to stay exactly as they are. Since we came to Shanghai eight years ago we have moved six times.

My sister says that I'm growing up. She looks at my crib. She tells me that when we move we are going to share a room and a big bed until she gets married, and after that I'll have everything to myself. It won't be long. Then she glances around and adds that I won't be playing with dolls much longer.

"Why does Uncle Ernest want to economize?" I ask. "I thought Maria Mikhailovna inherited a fortune."

She did, my sister explains to me, but it appears that they have been overspending. Most of the fortune's gone, she says. They have to sell their car and Maria Mikhailovna has already sold a lot of her jewellery. They both have to get jobs.

I have heard Aunt Lena call Maria Mikhailovna foolish and wickedly wasteful. Could she be right perhaps? I only think of Maria Mikhailovna as generous. But alas, her generosity is now causing me unspeakable grief.

At dinner my mother and sister try to cheer me up but my father doesn't say very much. He looks at me sympathetically over his bortsch. He doesn't seem very enthusiastic about the move himself. But then my father is not a person easily moved to enthusiasms, my mother has sometimes upbraided him for worrying too much and being a tiresome wet blanket.

I go to bed early. My sister's words ring in my mind as I curl up in my crib. She said that I wouldn't be playing with dolls much longer.

I know she is right. I don't know any grownups who play with dolls. My sense of desolation is compounded. This is the first time I have actually faced the fact that I'm growing up, that indeed my doll-playing days will soon be over. I can't imagine what life will be like without them. Every Saturday morning I redress my dolls in fresh clothes, washing, and later ironing, the ones I have taken off. I tell them everything. I re-enact for them all that happens to me. What will I do without them? Life stretches before me, a vast wilderness of empty years. Watching the moonlight shine on my triangular blue vase, I think about the adults I know. I see their lives too as vast empty wildernesses. What interest can life possibly hold if you can't share your doings with a group of understanding dolls?

I fall into a troubled sleep and in the morning I wake to misery. At school I tell Louba the bad news. For the first time in my life I don't want to go home from school. I am now old enough to travel on the tram by myself and I sit dolefully as the tram clanks its way home. As soon as I arrive my mother and I set out for the new house.

In the years to come, lodged in the substructure of my psyche, there will be a house of stairs. Steep stairs, dim, uncarpeted, echoing. A house whose rooms are incidental to the concept of stairs, a madman's fantasy of levitation.

And soaring up and catapulting down will be a twelve-year-old, caught in that fantasy of perpetual motion. The banisters fly past, the walls slide by, the child climbs endlessly, drops mindlessly, trapped as inexorably as Alice in her dream. "I want to buy a bungalow," I will cry to my husband years later, but the twelve-year-old coursing up and down in my blood will laugh. You will never escape, she will say.

My mother and I take a bus to Avenue Haig. We come to a large, cement complex of narrow terrace houses. We walk down a long lane, No. 159. My mother takes out a key and unlocks a door numbered 14 and we enter the empty house at Victory Terrace.

We walk across an entrance hall toward the first ground-floor room, and at once I am lost in stairs. I stand at the bottom of a well and I look up into a chimerical network of steps and banisters. The ceiling at the top of the house vanishes in shadows, it is so remote it could have its being among thunderclouds. My mother sweeps me up flight after flight, I glimpse an apologetic room at each landing, pathetic victims of an architectural lunacy. She hustles me to the sixth floor and propels me out on to a roof garden. We stand, catching our breaths, the city crouching below us, while hatred for the house slowly fills me, like a miasma creeping through my blood.

I see that this complex called Victory Terrace is very large and my mother tells me it is owned by a sect of Belgian monks whose monastery is situated in the centre of the compound. I can glimpse it among its trees. No trees soften the concrete of Victory Terrace. I think of the monks next door to my school. Are these monks giving their lives to God too? Opposite our house is a long row of garages and a machine shop. The machine shop houses the works for an artesian well that will provide water for the complex. Mother explains that this water is better and safer for us to drink than the municipal water. She also tells me with triumph in her voice that we will now have a telephone, something we have never had before. As we descend the stairs she explains the sleeping arrangements, but I'm not listening, the dim, windowless stairwell fills me with despair.

At home I appeal to my sister to persuade Mother to change her mind, but she tells me that everything has already been settled. She is looking forward to her fiancé's dismissal from the sanatorium. He's going back to his studies so that he can become a health inspector with the Shanghai Municipal Council. As soon as he gets his certificate they will be married. I'm glad for my sister, but the thought of the new house acts like a giant paperweight on my spirits.

In addition to the sheer ugliness of the house, my whole being rebels against living with someone else again. I have learned to treasure privacy. Though I have become fond of Uncle Ernest and Maria Mikhailovna, I know our home will never be our own any more. And the new school fills me with apprehension.

Mother arranges for the move to take place when I'm away at school. I do not see the furniture carried out of my beloved Sun Avenue home.

On the day of the move I am told to go straight to the new house after school. Maria Mikhailovna and Uncle Ernest have already moved in and there is tea laid on in the ground floor dining-room with little store-bought cakes. Our dining-room furniture looks out of place. There is an arcola stove in the middle of the right hand wall. It is painted a vulgar silver and dominates the room. This stove will heat the water in the radiators throughout the house, a new feature. French windows at the far end of the dining-room lead to a tiny fenced-in yard. The kitchen opens from the hall beside the dining-room, and above the kitchen, up a flight of stairs, is a room for the servants.

Maria Mikhailovna offers herself as a tour guide so that I can see the arrangements in the rest of the house. I am not enthusiastic but appreciate her offer, she is the only person who makes one. We walk up the stairs past the first bathroom and to the sitting-room directly above the dining-room. This room has Uncle Ernest's furniture in it. Unfamiliar couches and soft chairs are ranged around the room, only our gramophone stands in the corner. I feel a wrench in my heart when I see it. I'm sure it doesn't like the new room any more than I do. Maria Mikhailovna tells me she has many records that I will simply love.

Farther up, on the same landing as the second bathroom, is the bedroom my sister and I will share until she is married. It is long and narrow, dominated at one end by a large white wardrobe with an oval mirror. The wardrobe towers over the room and has a projecting ornamental cornice disguising storage space for light paraphernalia. At the other end of the room, by the window, is a matching dressing-table with a large square mirror, swinging, rather unnervingly, on a set of hinges, and small shelves on either side fitted with jewellery drawers. The dresser sits on tall, thin legs and has leaves and flowers outlined in gold around the mirror and the drawers. My heart sinks when I look at this furniture. Was it another auction bargain?

Against one wall stands a bed with a metal frame painted white. Space is limited so everything is crowded together. I see that Mother has placed my bamboo table with my Bible and my blue triangular vase on the wall opposite the bed, but I realize that there is no room for my black wicker trunk and my dolls. Although I shouldn't want to have them around, my heart turns over with disappointment, but I'm ashamed to ask about them.

Maria Mikhailovna and I ascend to the fifth floor where she and Uncle Ernest have settled in. They have a set of modern furniture, a pale gold wood. The dresser is low, with an inset in the centre where you can sit on a padded stool to make yourself look beautiful. There is a three-way mirror so that you can see your reflection at every angle.

We ascend the last flight of stairs to the topmost floor, and there on the final landing is my black wicker trunk with my dolls. My mother has set them all up just like I had them in my room in Sun Avenue. The last bedroom, atop mine and my sister's, is my parents'. I step out on to the roof garden as I did on my first visit to the house and look across the roof of the building with the artesian well to the monastery. Two monks are strolling between the trees, with their books clasped to their chests, giving their lives to God. I have heard my father say that the houses are profitable for the monks. Is that the way they are giving their lives to God? My hostility wafts across to the monastery garden and alights on the heads of the strolling monks. In my heart I call down vengeance on those pious heads. It is as if I know already that in an angry, resentful corner of my psyche I shall always live in this place of ill design, dark staircases and a lowering sense of doom.

We return downstairs to where Uncle Ernest is jolly over tea and cakes. Maria Mikhailovna tells Mother that she has arranged for a houseboy. He is fresh from the country and can't speak any English, but will learn. His name is Ah Foh.

Maria Mikhailovna is very kind to me. She says I can sit at her dressing-table whenever I like and use her elegant silver-backed comb and brushes. She tells me my hair is beautiful, platinum blond she calls it, and says that actresses in Hollywood would give their right arms for hair like mine. I doubt that but feel flattered. She promises to knit me a sweater, powder blue she says, of angora wool. I admire a ring on her hand, a thin gold band set with an emerald. She takes it off and gives it to me. It's a real emerald. I can't believe it. My mother protests, but Maria Mikhailovna reminds my mother that the ring is hers to give away. Though my mother does not reply I know she is thinking that this is how Maria Mikhailovna disburdened herself of her fortune. I imagine this is true, but on the other hand she must have made many people happy. Later, up in her room, she gives me a tiny bottle of perfume. My mother does not approve of the gift of perfume and I compromise by keeping it on my dresser and only sniffing it from time to time. And yet all this attention from Maria Mikhailovna does not reconcile me to the loss of my Sun Avenue home and my very own room, and I can't forget that my present misery is due to her undisciplined generosity.

The days pass and we settle into Victory Terrace. Maria Mikhailovna buys two greyhound puppies. My mother is alarmed. She has not been consulted. To my mother's relief it is soon discovered that the puppies cannot negotiate the stairs. Their back legs are too long. The puppies are given to the Canidrome to be trained for the dog races. My mother's relief is short-lived. Maria Mikhailovna immediately procures a Great Dane.

I adore Ledda. I take her for walks, or perhaps she takes me. With a dog like that I'm queen of the terrace. Nobody dares to cross me. Ledda loves me as much as I love her. She waits for me to come home from school and leaps up at me to lick me all over my face. Ledda personifies pure joy. I feel I can almost forgive Maria Mikhailovna, but I don't, quite.

I ask my mother if I can have my dolls back in my room when my sister leaves to get married. I still hanker after them. My mother says nobody knows when my sister is going to get married. She certainly doesn't. She sounds brusque, almost harsh.

One day there is a lot of talk among the grownups. It is about the wedding. I can see a disagreement is brewing. I take refuge in the room I share with my sister, sit down on the bed and cover my ears. I hate disagreements among the people I love best. Suddenly there is an emergency. My mother is ill. People are running up and down the stairs. She thinks she is having a heart attack. My doctor uncle is summoned.

My doctor uncle arrives very soon and attends my mother. When he comes out of my parents' bedroom he walks down the stairs talking to my father. I hear him say that my mother has had an anxiety attack. There is nothing wrong with her heart. He thinks she should stop fussing about the wedding.

I am not consoled. I wonder if my doctor uncle could be mistaken and if she will die. Terror grips me. For the first time in my life I see my mother as a real person subject to dangers. I sit on the bed, my mind zeroing in on my parents. They have been there as far back as I can remember. Now, in the course of a few moments, I suddenly realize that they will not always be there. They might die at any time. Tonight, tomorrow. My terror grows.

In the bathroom Maria Mikhailovna is measuring out valerian drops into a glass of water for my mother. I love the smell of valerian, it represents a bulwark against panic, anxiety, perhaps even death. I beg her to give me some as well and she complies, with a drop or two. They are delicious.

That night my sister comes to bed in great distress and as I lie beside her I blame the whole incident on the heavy, brooding house. Such things never happened on Sun Avenue.

Chapter Eight

In Vancouver, in the supernatural eighties, I take my aunt shopping.

"When you go to the big mall, take me with you," my aunt often says to me. Her eagerness to see the shops and to find out what people are doing warms me. Her enthusiasm is boundless, her wonder great. The quantity of merchandise amazes her. She shakes her head on which her silver wig sits becomingly. The size of the place baffles her. You could put the whole of downtown Kronstadt into this mall, she tells me, and still have space left over. I put my hand under her elbow. Her head reaches just above my shoulder. We chat as we walk, our Russian conversation going much like this:

"Why are you holding me up?" she asks me. "I can walk by myself, you know."

"I'm not holding you *up,*" I say, "I'm just holding you because I love you."

She squeezes my hand in quick remorse and laughs in a small amused burst. I love these short bursts of her laughter, reminiscent of youth, joy. They ambush your heart.

"Remember how I used to pick you up at school?" she says.

"You didn't like to let go of *my* hand," I remind her.

"You weren't my child. I felt more responsible for you."

"You used to bring me Sunkist oranges when I was sick. Remember? I loved them but they were very expensive."

"They were good for you," she replies, discounting the kindness.

"You did so much for us," I say. "You and Uncle Kolya." Uncle Kolya, my doctor uncle. His full name was Nicolai Nicolaivich Kusnetzov, a name deeply respected in the community.

"Everyone does what they can," she says. But I know that's not quite true. Everyone doesn't, but she does.

"It was good living in the Far East," she says. There is nostalgia in her voice.

"Not for everyone," I say. "It was never easy for my dad."

"Your father found it hard to cope," she says. "He was a disappointed man. I think he never got over the shock of losing everything. Fifty-two's too old to start all over again. He became a very anxious man. Too anxious."

"Yes, he was," I agree. "I never thought too much about him when I was growing up. I guess kids don't. He was simply there. But I loved him dearly."

"He was a good husband and father," my aunt says. "Always concerned. He *cared* about what might happen to each one of you. We all cared about one another. No-one *cares* any more." She often says this. Then something catches her eye and she changes the subject. "Look, there's the dress I saw the other day. It's still in the window."

"Come on, try it on," I urge her.

"Do you think I should?" she asks. "Don't you think it's silly for an old woman to be buying new clothes?"

"No, I don't," I say. "Come on." The truth is that to me she isn't an old woman, to me she is timeless. She lives in time but is not of it. Her interest in living is inspiring. Two years ago, at 91, she took a trip to Europe. Her spunk has outwitted time—that rock beneath her ribs. She often says she would like to go to the moon, that if she were young she'd have wanted to be an astronaut. We do not honestly believe her, but she means it and I must add this. Some years later, when my aunt does die, a quiet, dignified passing, Nina, on exploring an old cookbook, finds all the news items regarding the exploration of space carefully cut out and saved at the back of the cookbook.

We buy the dress she fancies.

On the way home we are both quiet. She is tired now. My thoughts fly back. Yes, they all cared, the grownups among whom I lived. They cared about one another. When we moved away from Sun Avenue and settled in Victory

Terrace, a significant change began to take place in my inner life.

The change involved growing awareness and the concerns that dog it. Up to this time my parents had been hazy figures conveniently inhabiting the dream world that was my childhood. Now they began to emerge in my mind as people in their own right. Earlier I had been more impressed with other people than with my parents. They had simply always been there, warm, comforting presences, appearing more as extensions of my own existence than as separate beings. I was jolted out of this trance by my mother's anxiety attack and the panic it generated among the adults, bringing to mind the death of the landlady in our east end house and the terror of the coffin. It gradually dawned upon me that my mother was not immortal, nor my father either. I began to recognize their importance to me, and their fragility, to value these two people whom I had been taking so much for granted.

Most of all about my mother I remember her hands, sometimes red-knuckled from washing, at other times floured from kneading dough, occasionally smelling of onions, though more often creamed and perfumed and manicured, highlighted by rings saved from better times, mixing tiles in a mah-jong game, but always moving. A small, slimly rounded woman, with a proud lilt to her head and with well-shaped, endlessly busy hands.

And I remember her laugh, a gentle laugh, escaping frequently. She needed all the good humour she could muster, for my father was pessimistic and inclined toward hypochrondria. As my aunt had said, his anxiety was for us. We had no security of any kind outside of his earning power. If anything happened to him we would be waifs in a large, uncaring city. Although my mother was a shrewd and competent housekeeper, able to eke out slender means so that we wanted for nothing, she had no money-earning skills. She was the daughter who had stayed home to help with the needs of the family.

My father's defeatist tendencies often irked my mother, but she was grateful that he didn't break altogether under his responsibilities as so many other refugees from the revolution did. To be forced out of affluence and familiar surroundings, to lose the accumulations of a lifetime and to start again at an advanced age in an alien and indifferent environment, took courage and devotion. He was a man of deep integrity. These were all fine but weighty qualities, and his temperament sagged under them. My mother had to deal with it. She was thirteen years his junior and she longed for lightness, gaiety, joy. He adored her but could not give her these things. She once shocked Aunt Lena by saying that if she could live her life over again, she would choose to be a highly paid courtesan.

My mother used to say that when she woke up in the morning there were birds singing in her heart. She would tell me that I and my sister could be Estonian princesses and suggested that I behave as if I were. She dreamed dreams, none of which came true, but she never stopped dreaming them. Proud of her looks, she was coquettish right to the end, adoring admiration.

She made us feel somehow that our less than affluent situation in the world was temporary, that that was not how things were supposed to be. That we had all been born to a better fate than our ignominious victimization by the revolution. Lack of affluence, insecurity, were the lot of others, we should somehow be exempt. She walked with a straight back and a light step, her head held high. It was a very pretty head.

My father was a plodder. He plodded to work and he plodded home. He walked with his hands in his pockets and his head bent. He always wore a hat. He was conscious of his ears, which he thought were too big. Hair sprouted from them and had to be regularly removed. He blamed this strange growth on a Japanese barber who had once shaved the insides of his ears, though my mother did not hold with this belief. He had a large head with a prominent, broad forehead and a heavy nose that grew more substantial with the years. His hair was thin and straight, sandy in colour. He was a homely man, but to us, his loved ones, his face was beautiful because we never experienced anything but kindness at his hands.

My father found it difficult to join Mother in her flights of fancy and romance. Only once a week, on Saturday night, when he allowed himself a few glasses of vodka with his dinner, which was usually his favourite pork chops, did his heavily jowled face break into relaxed smiles and he found himself able to enter into mother's world of lightness and gaiety. Then he would compliment and kiss her, and us into the bargain, and she would glow with pleasure. But to me those Saturday nights were disturbing. The conviviality seemed spurious. I preferred my father to be his everyday gloomy self. The gloom did not obscure his kindness and that was all that mattered to me.

Although the artificial glow produced by the Saturday night vodka made me uncomfortable, I understood from my mother that it was one of the things that were necessary to a man. She made a clear distinction between men and women. She never considered herself of less value than a man, but different, quite different, maybe even a cut above. Men were useful, she said, but there were also some things we women just had to put up with if we had a male connection, as most of us did.

One of the earliest things I remember associated with my father and the male connection was his penknife. It was broad with a grey-and-black corrugated handle and two blades, one short and wide, the other longer, narrower. It also had a corkscrew and was much in demand at parties where wine was served. My main interest in this knife was the way my father sharpened my pencils with it. He would place the pencil against the thumb of his left hand and draw the short blade firmly but carefully toward the tip. Short curls of wood fell away revealing at last a perfect point. My father sharpened his pencils at work in this way too, and his thumb was permanently blackened by the ingrained lead. But well-sharpened pencils were indispensable to life. Even when pencil sharpeners made their appearance he continued to sharpen pencils in his own way. They were always exactly right and the lead never chipped as it often did in the new-fangled invention. I never learned the knack of sharpening pencils that way.

The other thing I remember in regard to the masculine factor in our lives was the smell of nicotine that permeated my father's whole person. He smoked incessantly and when I was bidden to look for something in one of his jacket pockets, my fingers always encountered a layer of tobacco at the bottom. Mother used to empty the tobacco out of the window, pocket by pocket, before she sent his coats to the cleaners, tightening her lips and shaking her head in disapproval. But I never heard her suggest that he should stop smoking.

Although so much of value had been snatched away by the revolution, my father had one consolation, the encyclopaedia he had brought out of Russia. It had cost him luggage space and money he could ill afford, but the treasure had proved to be well worth the sacrifice. The twelve volumes were bound in leather, elegantly illustrated, new, up to date. They were in German. My father spoke German fluently as he did Russian and English, French and his native Estonian. At that time the Germans were the acknowledged leaders in the organization of knowledge.

The encyclopaedia and all it symbolized began to loom large in my life in the new house. Perhaps with life's realities of change and transience suddenly crowding in upon me I found it necessary to cling to something that offered indestructible comforts. During the first terrible, sad years of loss and displacement, the encyclopaedia had been my father's escape from desolation. General knowledge was a source of limitless fascination for him and he read the great tomes whenever he wasn't too tired. We grew to depend upon his remarkable memory for everything we wanted to know. Now, in Victory Terrace, I became aware of the encyclopaedia as an integral part of my father's life.

In the evenings he would sit in his brown chair by the ugly silver arcola, his thin thighs, clad in shabby trousers, pressed close together to support the weight of the volume on his lap, and read steadily, always dampening his finger at his lips to turn the fine, gold-edged paper. Later he wore a pair of glasses that left creases on his baggy cheeks when he took them off. The books embodied self-preservation.

It was on Victory Terrace, when the dream world of my childhood had been invaded by hard reality, that the acquisition and preservation of knowledge became my escape and salvation too. On those evenings when my father was not too tired to translate and share with me the marvels of the encyclopaedia, I forgot the ugliness of the house in which I was condemned to live, I forgot the awesome prospect of the new school. I followed his finger along the alien words, listened to his voice interpreting them, feasted my eyes on the elaborate coloured plates, and I was happy.

My mother respected, but was not entranced by the encyclopaedia. Whenever she had a free moment she would take her sewing or her knitting and sit down to listen to the radio. She loved music, the light operas and waltzes in particular, and she would go around the house humming, perhaps living once again in that world of romance and pleasure from which she had been so rudely separated. The gramophone that had been placed in the sitting-room filled with Uncle Ernest's furniture, was now equipped with the new steel needles that had recently come on the market, but my mother liked the radio better. It was handier, there was more variety, records were expensive and we did not have many. So she listened to her music in preference to partaking of the joys of the encyclopaedia.

But neither did she discourage me from spending hours immersed in those wonderful books. In her own way she was proud of my father's knowledge, proud that I was absorbing some of it too, and absorbing it I certainly was. History, literature and philosophy were only glimmerings in my mind at that time, but my acquaintance with them grew rapidly under my father's guidance. He would expound on the insights of the poets and the novelists, the brilliance of the great philosophers and the highlights of world history of which latter we learned very little at our English school. A good deal of what he spoke of was beyond my comprehension and he warned me of this, but I loved to listen to him, just to hear the magic words rolling off his tongue. I became familiar with all the famous names and looked forward to the time when I would be able to read all those works for myself, and to understand their mysteries.

He was not only a repository for useful facts, he was also a thinker. He spent a great deal of his time on Sunday, his only day off, lying on his bed with his arms crossed behind his head and resting on the low iron rail of the bedstead. Mother direfully predicted that he would lose the hair on the back of his head but he never did, although he did wear away the white paint which covered the iron rail. A stretch of black metal testified to his ruminations. Although he could not join my mother in her flights of romantic fancy, he had his own escape into the world of imagination.

He would lie for hours staring out of the window, up at the sky, pondering the problems of the world and of the universe, and coming up with ideas, most of which he kept to himself. I would sometimes catch him with a small secret look of amusement on his face. This look was different both from the look of gloom he usually wore on his plodding path to and from work and also from the look of slightly inebriated affection he displayed on his vodka evenings, but it was the look I liked best.

Sometimes, while my mother played mah-jong with the ladies in the sitting-room, he would tell me some of the theories that he had come up with lying there on his bed. Once, probably for lack of a better audience, he tried to explain to me, unsuccessfully, the principle of jet propulsion. Another time he said, "Men will walk on the moon in your lifetime." I remember hugging him, laughing, a little impatient of such excesses of fantasy. Yet another theory he cherished had to do with the possibility of recalling the earth's past from the depths of space. He theorized that if light indeed curved it should be possible to capture images of events long gone. "We should be able to witness the whole of the Hundred Years War," he said once, adding with a dry little chuckle "had any one of us a hundred years to do it in!" And one afternoon he told me that one day I would be able to see pictures of events on the other side of the world at the moment of their happening. "How, Father, how?" I cried, fascinated, but also a little worried about his sanity and glad that Mother was playing mah-jong and was out of earshot of his wild imaginings.

Once he repeated his conviction about the men on the moon at a dinner table. H.G. Wells had written a novel about such an adventure. It was one of those sumptuous Russian dinners beginning with hors d'oeuvres and proceeding through fish and meat pies, roast pheasants and whipped cream desserts, all helped down with a generous supply of vodka. There were loud guffaws about the men on the moon. Someone suggested that another glass of vodka might bring forth even more electrifying prophesies. My father had laughed too, good-naturedly, but my mother was embarrassed almost to tears and I quailed lest he reveal the idea of viewing the happenings on the other side of the world. At home Mother told him that if he ever talked nonsense like that again, humiliating her in front of all her friends, she would never go to another party with him. He did not interrupt her while she spoke, waiting till her tirade was over, and then he smiled wryly and said, "But they will, you know."

This new awareness of my parents as distinct individuals rather than projections of myself brought its own grief, a new overriding concern. I went through a period of almost pathological anxiety. After my mother's attack I would come home from school with fear chilling my heart. I would call out to her at once and her answer would assuage my fear, but only till the next day. In the evening I was on tenterhooks awaiting my father's return and endured agonies if he chanced to be late. On one such occasion I walked down to the bus-stop to ease my tension and was just in time to see him getting off the bus, stoop-shouldered in his shabby coat, his hat pulled low over his head to disguise the big ears. No figure in the world could have been dearer or more welcome. My relief at seeing him was like an explosion in my chest. I ran toward him, shouting, scaring him half to death with my joy.

Chapter Nine

My participation in two Christmases every year made me the envy of my classmates. My Lutheran parents celebrated Christmas Eve on 24 December and my Aunt Lena and her doctor celebrated the Russian Orthodox Christmas on 7 January.

Although in the east end and on Sun Avenue our Christmas celebrations were modest because means were scanty, nonetheless a tree, however unassuming, simple gifts and a small dinner for Nina and her parents were sufficient to fill my eager soul with anticipation and delight. How much more exciting then was the celebration at my aunt's house.

Christmas day on the seventh was Nina's day in their family and there was always a large party with many children. The glittering tree stood in the centre of the sitting-room and reached to the ceiling. It was the hub of Christmas. Under it lay the mysterious parcels that we children coveted. Around it we danced, dressed in our best clothes, sang old Russian songs and played games. But the highlight of the evening for me was a huge crêpe paper bag of bonbons I was given to take home along with one of the gifts from under the tree. These bags stood in a bristling row on the mantelpiece, tied with festive ribbons, and contained a wealth of candy, fruit and nuts. To explore my bag at home and to look forward to treats for days to come was pure bliss. In spite of the intervening years, I can still feel that rush of joy at the rustle of crêpe paper.

But the two Christmases I enjoyed, even if envied by my friends, had a side effect. Though no significance was attached by either family to the differing dates, the discrepancy puzzled and disturbed me. How could there be two dates for Jesus' birth? One of them had to be wrong. I did not know it then, but the ground that seemed so solid under my feet was already starting to unsettle.

Today I sit on the chesterfield in Nina's elegant condo, holding a cup of tea in my hands and a cake plate on my lap. My aunt is wearing the dress we bought in the mall. When she speaks her voice has a hint of nostalgia, her Russian words are plaintive.

"They are all gone," she says shaking her head, "all gone." She wonders why she's still here. Where's my hair, she asks. She's deaf and tired. It's even hard to lift a kettle these days. "And they, they are all gone."

"But you still like to go shopping," I tease. She smiles, almost impishly, shrugs, head a little askew.

She is referring to her family of course, all those brothers and sisters. She agrees that she still likes to do things, but she wants to know why we all have to lose so much as we grow older. She complains about how ugly she's become.

"You're not ugly," I say, meaning it. She is a delicate Dresden lady. She ignores me and pursues her reflections. She feels God and Nature have made a mess between them. She could have done a better job, she thinks. It would have made more sense if we could stay as we were and then just drop dead.

A year or two ago a strange thing happened. After my grandfather brought his family from Kronstadt to Vladivostok to take up his new position in the courts of law, the eldest son, the star Alexander, who had been left behind, had married. He was still in the west therefore when the revolution broke out, in the forefront of the civil war. They heard from him spasmodically. Then the letters ceased. They heard neither from him nor from his family. When my Aunt Lena and my mother left Vladivostok for Shanghai there had been no news of any kind, and later, when my Uncle Ernest came out to Shanghai, and, still later, when Aunt Lida came out in the thirties, there was still nothing. Gradually a veil was drawn over his memory. It was presumed that Alexander had perished in the civil war along with thousands of others and was never to be seen again by his adoring family.

And now, recently, an acquaintance brought my aunt a newspaper clipping from Paris. It was an obituary. It said that Colonel Alexander Yacub had died in Paris. He left behind him sons and daughters. He was in his late nineties.

My aunt agonized. To think that they had been in China all those years and Alexander, miraculously escaped from the Reds, had been living in Paris, and neither group had known about the other. The pathos and irony tortured her for days. She still tells me about it as if I had not heard. All those years, and *we never knew,* she says.

"They are all gone," she says yet again, intertwining her fingers and turning her palms upwards in a gesture of hopelessness.

It might seem strange, but I never feel that they are all gone—my mother and father and the grave doctor, my jolly if misguided Uncle Ernest, sardonic Aunt Lida brought out of Russia for a price, the controversial and passionate Maria Mikhailovna. In my mind they move around me as before, intent on their own affairs. I can see them all as they were at the first Christmas Eve we celebrated in Victory Terrace.

On that Christmas Eve my parents could afford to be more expansive. Father had just received a substantial raise, an unprecedented event. I remember the pleasure on his homely face when he told my mother the good news, and how they had had a glass of wine to celebrate. I watched them in wonder for I had never seen them drink wine without an occasion like New Year's Eve. I sipped a bit from Mother's glass, relishing the ambrosial taste of celebration.

As usual she and I had gone a couple of days before Christmas Eve to buy a tree, except that this year the tree was grander, taller, thicker. As always we brought it home on a rickshaw, walking beside it, but this year we had gone with Ah Foh, our new houseboy. He had haggled for us and was pleased with the price he had wrung out of the tree merchant. We set it up with his help and decorated it, carefully fastening the candleholders with their four-inch candles to the prickly boughs. Ledda leaped around us in delight to the great peril of the tree and Mother's annoyance, and finally had to be hauled off by Ah Foh and shut up in the kitchen where she howled woefully.

Ah Foh grinned and co-operated with us eagerly in everything. He had come straight from the country knowing no English but in no time at all he had learned enough to be able to discuss meals and household chores easily. He learned the rudiments of electricity and plumbing and he even began to offer bits of well-meaning and useful advice. When I started to sprout in my early teens and was all legs and elbows he told Mother that I read too much, that reading made me too thin. He offered to buy us rice from the

Chinese city where it was much cheaper, for the compradores in the Settlement shops marked up commodities unscrupulously, and he bought our vegetables for us from his friends in the Chinese market at a great saving too. My mother grew more and more dependent on him and when he got a bargain, his face, with its great, flashing grin full of crooked yellow teeth, was a treat to see.

So that Christmas Ah Foh, delighted with his bargaining, had entered fully into the spirit of the occasion, although our custom of bringing a dead tree into the house and decorating it must have seemed bizarre to him. There was a curious sense of insularity about our Christmas. We were celebrating an esoteric festival while the vast majority hosting us in this alien land was cool and skeptical and sometimes derisive. As I walked home from church on Christmas Eve, my heart full of the joy of Christmas, I was conscious of the silent, closed stores, the darkened houses of the thousands who were significantly unimpressed. It never failed to depress and confuse me.

Earlier in the day I had helped Mother wrap gifts for the relatives. In the days before scotch tape it took two to make a good-looking package, one to hold the paper down at the ends, the other to tie the ribbon. That evening we placed the gifts beneath the tree, the goose in the oven, Ah Foh was instructed on the basting procedures, Mother reminded him to wear his new gown, and she, Father and I departed for the German Lutheran Church for the candlelight service. My sister, grownup and engaged, no longer came with us.

The German Lutheran Church was the only Lutheran church in the city and of course my father felt at home in it. Neither my mother nor I understood a word, but the carols were familiar and the atmosphere of the evening service was reverent and aesthetically impeccable. It had been the highlight of my year even when we attended a small church in the east end, but this year we went to the new German Church, an imposing edifice that had been built just a block away from Victory Terrace. There was a tree rising to the top of the nave, sublime in gold and silver, shining with a hundred white tapers, the only tree I had ever seen that surpassed Aunt Lena's tree in sheer glory. The tapers were electric, but so craftily designed that to this day they pose in my mind as real candles. I certainly thought they were real then, and never wondered as to how it was that they never wavered and never grew any shorter.

The church was warm and smelled of evergreens. While the minister droned on I thought of the goose cooking in the oven and the gifts we had placed under the tree. I wondered what my gifts would be. The singing of the carols filled me with a bursting joy. I had no idea that the time was approaching when my father would turn sadly away from the German church, never to enter its doors again. But no-one thought of the possibility of war when we first moved to Victory Terrace. That hour in church on Christmas Eve stands out in memory as the cosiest, safest, most pleasurable hour of my whole year.

So on this first Christmas at Victory Terrace we return from church and the house smells of the tree and of the goose in the oven. Ah Foh is grinning like a great sun at the door of the kitchen, resplendent in his new gown, and the relatives start to arrive.

The first to come are Aunt Lena and the doctor, and Nina, now nearly sixteen and sporting a new pair of shoes with that eye-catching feature, a small high heel. I admire her, long for the years to pass. Nina's dress is fashionable and her long plaits have been attractively pinned up. Aunt Lena takes off the silver-fox fur fastened over her coat and asks me to take it upstairs to my mother's bedroom and lay it carefully on the bed. I run upstairs nuzzling the fur. It's wondrously soft and smells of perfume. It makes me sneeze. I lay it carefully on Mother's bed and stroke it for a few moments, wishing it were still alive. Then I skip downstairs again.

The doctor smiles, nodding his greetings, but he has not

totally relinquished the underlying gravity. Softly spoken and slow-moving, dark, curly hair and moustache carefully groomed, outfitted in a sombre suit, he puts on his glasses and examines our tree, standing with his hands behind his back. I wonder if he is comparing it, unfavourably, with the trees he has had in his own home. For a moment I wish our decorations were more elaborate, but then he says, "very beautiful" and my small heart fills with joy.

With Nina and Aunt Lena has come Aunt Lida. Aunt Lida is a newcomer to the family. She has recently been bought out of the Soviet Union by Aunt Lena. I know the story of her youth, of her tragic romance. She should be such a figure of romance, tall and pale and beautiful, but she's nothing like that. She is small and plump and pink-cheeked, and over the years has become rather plain although she was pretty enough once as I know by her photographs. She laughs often. Later when I am older, I will notice that her laugh has an edge to it, that it holds irony rather than humour. She fascinates me with her tales of the Terror, of knockings on the door in the dead of night, shoot-outs in the streets, of jewellery skilfully hidden in bars of soap, of endless queues for food, starvation victims, people vanishing forever. It is from her that we have heard of how my Uncle Vladimir, the less than favourite son, pulled them through the worst times by plying his chosen trade—Vladimir, the dropout and the rebel, whose apprenticeship to a shoemaker had appalled the upper middle-class family and all their friends. She has told us how she herself had had to put her talent with the needle to more practical use than the embroidery at which she had always excelled. She has become a skilled and resourceful seamstress.

She too has a fox fur, but hers is red and she doesn't bother to send it upstairs with me but hangs it up in the hall over her coat. The tail hangs down disconsolately. She mounts the stairs to the sitting-room and sinks down on the couch, folding her hands in her lap. On her finger I see a ring set with small diamonds and rubies, the engagement ring she saved from the Terror. Now she lives with Aunt Lena and helps out in the household. She sews for all of us, taking pleasure and pride in her work, designing her own patterns.

Aunt Lena is bustling and practical. She offers to help my mother and follows her down to the kitchen.

I follow too because I love to see the great goose basted, its brown flesh bursting with fat, the savoury steam escaping in a hot cloud, to catch a glimpse of the roasting potatoes and apples sizzling in their pan. My mouth waters shamelessly. As I watch the marvellous operation, I hear a bit of gossip.

My Aunt Lena says that there has been another row.

Yes, Mother says, Aunt Lena must have been right all along.

Aunt Lena shrugs, her lips compressed.

Mother points out that it is, after all, Ernest's life. That he chose it.

Mysteriously my aunt warns my mother not to let it become *her* life. A person who is being so unreasonable is hard to handle. My mother must think of her own health.

They are talking about Uncle Ernest and Maria Mikhailovna.

My curiosity is unbounded, although I hate to hear of troubles among the people I love. But I know there *has* been trouble. Lately I'm sure I've heard Maria Mikhailovna crying in her room, although I pretended to myself that I had imagined it.

Mother reassures my aunt about her health while poking at the potatoes in the oven. She sounds a bit miffed. If she made a mistake when she agreed to live with Uncle Ernest and Maria Mikhailovna, she may not want to hear about it. As for me, I'm dying to know what Maria Mikhailovna is being unreasonable about now. Is it still something to do with the lost fortune?

There are steps on the stairs, Uncle Ernest and Maria

Mikhailovna are coming down to join the party. The kitchen dialogue is cut off. Maria Mikhailovna carries gifts to put under the tree. I run up to the sitting-room and hover round the tree, wondering which packages are for me. The names are always hidden until the last moment. The adults sip wine. I have a new dress on, and although it has been made over from a dress Nina has outgrown, I'm delighted with it. Long white stockings (how I long for silk!) and black patent-leather shoes complete my outfit. I'm starving.

My sister comes down, her holiday finery very chic. She looks pretty and eager. The doorbell rings and she hurries to meet her expected guest, her fiancé. He has completely recovered from his illness. Briefly my anxiety surfaces, I hope Mother will not have another attack although it seems that she has accepted my sister's choice. Secretly and delightedly I applaud her good sense. My sister's fiancé looks very handsome indeed, like a movie star.

Our party is now complete.

At last the goose is ready and we all troop down to the dining-room. It is brought on to the table by Ah Foh in his new gown to exclamations of wonder, as if no-one has ever seen a goose before. Ah Foh nods and beams with pleasure, joyfully accepting the credit. The goose is brown and savoury and steaming. I offer my plate hopefully but Mother frowns at me. The guests must be served first. I hope there's enough for me.

There is enough. And there are loads of potatoes and apples and vegetables. Wine is passed around and as usual I get just a small glass and am told it is enough. The goose melts in my mouth. I could eat goose forever. But soon the plates are gathered up and we have dessert, little balls of egg-white floating in a thick custard sauce. Snowballs, they call it. Finally we are done and Ah Foh removes the plates, grinning. His large, yellow, higgledy-piggledy teeth fascinate me.

Now tea is being prepared in the kitchen in Mother's

large silver-plated samovar. And cakes are being brought to the table. Everyone exclaims again in wonder at these, and indeed Mother has outdone herself. There is fruit cake and chocolate torte and lovely, sticky, golden meringues. A bottle of liqueur is produced. Tiny glasses are set around it. But we're not starting on any of this yet. For now is the time to light the candles on the tree and hand out the gifts. We all mount to the sitting-room where Ledda is allowed to join us. Maria Mikhailovna speaks to her sharply and she lies down demurely. My father goes into the kitchen and returns with a bucket of water, which he sets down by the tree, the home emergency fire service. Then, ceremoniously striking a match, he lights the topmost candle. I beg him to let Nina and me light some of the others and he gives us each a lighted match, carefully supervising our efforts. When the last candle is lit, all the lamps are put out, and the tree stands, uplifted by the glory streaming from its branches. By the mystical light of the tree the gifts are distributed.

There are sweaters and gloves and scarves and belts and handkerchiefs and perfume and ornaments and books and pens and writing-paper. I sit, breath caught at each revelation, even though some of the gifts I have packed myself. My own gifts I put in a neat pile on the floor beside me. But when I open the gift Maria Mikhailovna has chosen for me, everything else is eclipsed. She has given me a necklace to match my dress. The stones flare like sunbursts in the light of the candles. I am speechless. I will love Maria Mikhailovna forever. How can she be unreasonable? Aunt Lena must be wrong.

Outside the stars pepper the sky. Under their light even the cement harshness of Victory Terrace is softened. I know the angels are singing.

Chapter Ten

The fun isn't over with Christmas Eve. The next day there will be the Christmas Day service at the Anglican Cathedral. The Cathedral will be heavily decorated with greens and candles, the Dean will be in his most festive robes, my heart will soar with the voices of the choir, and the pealing of the bells will send the message of Christ's birth to the farthest extremities of the city where so few have accepted him as king. And of course there will be more goodies, baked ham and Mother's specialty salads and the leftover cakes. And in a week's time we will have New Year's Eve with our traditional calendar-peeling ceremony, and a week after that will come Nina's Christmas with the party and the bags of bonbons. And throughout I will wear my sparkling new necklace. But beyond that, ah beyond that I don't want to look. Beyond that lies the new school.

Still, whether I want it to or not, time trips heedlessly by and I suddenly find all the joys are behind me and the bleakness of the new school is upon me.

My sister takes me to the school. I am dressed in my new uniform, navy blue with maroon tie and sash, and the prescribed blazer and beret, something I never had to wear before. And Aunt Lida and Mother between them have made me a warm navy blue coat, brand-new, not a hand-me-down. I also have a new attaché case for my books. It is brown and the locks snap smartly into place.

The school is a long, impressive, three-storeyed building with grey pebbled walls, white trim and brick facings. My sister guides me through the interview with the headmistress. She has my reports from my old school, but it is necessary to have tests before they can assign me to a class. My sister leaves and I am taken to an empty classroom. There I am given paper and pen and a question sheet. A teacher supervises me and when I am through I wait until she has marked my test. She seems pleased with the results and tells me I shall be in Form Four Lower. I am now free to go. School will start on the following day.

I wend my way down the stairs quite slowly. The school building is warm and I see it is heated by steam radiators, a rarity. The stairs are tiled. They have smooth banisters, nothing like the creaky splintery ones at my east-end school. I feel a little pang in my heart when I think of all my old friends left to cope with draughty corridors and chilly classrooms. Before leaving the school I look around outside. In the front flowerbeds run the length of the building, empty now of course in early January. I go around to the back and here playing-fields stretch in an expanse of winter-yellowed grass, bordered on the perimeter by shrubs and trees. In my old school the only bit of greenery we had was a tired-looking climbing wisteria over the front gate.

I arrive well before nine the next morning. It is a cold, rather rainy day and the girls are crowding into an entrance foyer, waiting for the school to open its doors. There's a dreadful din. I talk to a girl who's standing close to me, clutching her books to her chest. "I'm new" I say, "what happens when the doors open?" She stares at me and says solemnly, "They cut off our heads." I learn not to ask questions.

A bell sounds and the doors are opened by a Chinese boy wearing a white coat. The children surge in like a sea, I among them. They all head for the cloakrooms. I follow. I divest myself of my coat and change my shoes. Only runners are worn in the building. I follow the other girls to the assembly hall.

Assembly is held in the school auditorium, which doubles as a gym. It's twice the size of the hall at my old school where I had my famous success as Perseus. I am apprehended by a prefect and assigned to the right line.

There is a short talk by the headmistress to which I scarcely listen. I steal glances down the line of girls who are going to be my classmates. One or two glance back at me covertly. Another teacher gives out some notices and there is a short prayer addressed to no-one in particular, so none of the children leave in the way the Jewish girls had to leave at my old school. Then an older girl plays a lively march on the piano and we march out. I follow the girl in front of me asking no questions.

The school is spotless. Chinese "boys" in white gowns scurry around with mops and feather dusters. The classrooms are large and bright. Our home teacher is called Mrs. Close. She wears a fashionable outfit and lipstick.

At recess I follow the others down to the dining-room on the ground floor. I discover that buns and muffins are being sold but alas, I have no money. I salivate as the others chew all around me. No-one offers to buy me a bun or even to share one with me.

When the morning session is over I am famished. Everyone piles into the cloakrooms, pushing and shoving. I change as fast as I can and run almost all the way home.

As I approach our house the old fear suddenly envelops me. Is my mother dead?

She is not, and as quickly as it came the fear dissipates.

Ledda welcomes me with her deep-throated barking, nearly knocking me down in her excitement. I hug her great sturdy body. I am full of news. I talk without ceasing throughout lunch and beg Mother for money so that I can buy a bun at morning recess. I can't wait to go back to school. I forget how I hated the idea.

My desk is next to a Russian girl called Olga Sokoloff. She tells me her home is in the same direction as mine. Should we walk home together after school?

Olga is out-going, enthusiastic, very cheerful. She is looking forward to the tennis and hoping her mother can afford to buy her a racket. She lives a little further from the school than I do and we part at the corner. We promise to meet again the next morning at a quarter to nine on that same corner. Walking with Olga to and from school becomes a routine. We are enchanted with each other's company.

My absorption in school life is briefly interrupted by a great event. My sister is actually getting married. The ceremony will be at the Cathedral and I shall be a bridesmaid. I am to have a champagne beige silk dress, new, not a hand-me-down, black patent-leather shoes, and joy of joys, a pair of silk stockings.

My mother and my Aunt Lida have been working hard on the dresses for the wedding. Aunt Lida designs and cuts and Mother races her sewing-machine. It is hand-operated, and I help her. I twirl the handle while she holds the material for the long seams. Stop! my mother cries, and I stop the wheel instantly with my other hand, making a horrible slithering noise. Go! my mother orders and I twirl again as fast as I can till the spokes of the wheel become a blur.

My father, in an unprecedented move, orders a new suit.

The reception will be at my Aunt Lena's new apartment. Aunt Lena and my doctor uncle and Nina have moved again. Their complex is called Garden Apartments. The apartment has a fine entrance hall, large rooms and three bathrooms with hot water taps that always run hot water. At Victory Terrace we have hot water in the hot water taps only when the gas heater is lighted. There is another wonder, a refrigerator, the first I have ever seen. It is called a Frigidaire. There is also a new concept—clothes closets. My aunt and Nina will not have to use the old-fashioned wardrobes I hate so much. They will be able to hang their clothes and keep their shoes and hats on shelves in walk-in closets. I envy them the closets and the always available hot water.

The wedding will not be big but it will be chic. I like my sister's future husband more than ever and I'm glad my mother has stopped having palpitations about the marriage.

Although I am very happy for my sister, I'm even happier for myself. I shall now be able to have a room of my own again. With the preparations for the wedding everything has been in an uproar and our room in a muddle. Even at the best of times it would be hard to fit the possessions of two people successfully into one small room and my sister has been very patient with me. But when she leaves I can expand. I am beginning to recognize my deep need for order and for having things my own way. I experience some guilt about these feelings, but since my sister is going to be happy the guilt doesn't bite too deeply.

On her wedding day my sister wears a long white gown, a small hat over her freshly marcelled hair and a white fur jacket. She has a bouquet of roses, white lilies and trailing greenery. I've never seen anyone look more beautiful. I wonder if I will ever get married. It occurs to me that if I do I will have to share my bedroom with my husband. Would there be some way to avoid this?

There is a wedding lunch at my Aunt Lena's house. Everyone is in a happy mood. My sister and her new husband go off to the mountains for their honeymoon and I go off home to rearrange my belongings. I have been looking forward to this all through the ceremonies. I straighten the large bed that I will now have all to myself—I won't have to worry about wriggling or twiddling my toes any more. And then, sitting down on the bed, I suddenly feel very sad, and lonely for my sister.

Soon after the wedding I invite Olga to my house to meet my parents and in turn she invites me to hers. Olga's mother is a handsome, dark-haired woman with a musical voice. She is a singer, a rich contralto, and is able to accompany herself on the piano. She tells us about the good times they had in Russia, much in the manner of my own family. Olga's father is often ill so her mother is the chief breadwinner. She has a job in a department store but they cannot afford to have a servant on her salary. Olga often has to help out with the chores. I envy her when her mother lets her do some of the cooking. I'm seldom allowed in the kitchen.

Olga's father was an officer in the Tsar's army. He can't overcome his bitterness at the outcome of the revolution. His bitterness has made him ill. It is the same feeling I discern in my Aunt Lena's voice when she talks about the Bolsheviks.

Olga's house is also one in a row of terraces and it abuts on the Bubbling Well Cemetery. Although this cemetery is dominated by an Anglican chapel, any foreigner can be buried here, but no Chinese. It is the same with every public place in the city. The parks are only for foreigners, as is the Race Course, the restaurants, the clubs. Chinese are allowed in these places only in the role of servants. There are notices in some parks saying "No Chinese or dogs allowed." But there are Chinese diggers in the cemetery and Chinese gardeners.

Olga and I see nothing wrong with this order of things. In some curious way it has been made clear to us that the Chinese are not quite the same as we are, that they're not exactly regular people, but *Chinese.* Neither she nor I have any Chinese friends, and neither do our parents. Chinese are peasants out in the country, growing the rice and the vegetables we eat, and in the city they are labourers and tram drivers and shopkeepers, and they are servants. Everywhere, in hotels and theatres and schools and offices and private homes Chinese are servants. They are here to make life easier for us, to do all the unpleasant jobs. That's their *role.* We have no quarrel with that. We think that that is what Chinese *do.* Olga says the first thing she'll do when she grows up and gets a job will be to get a Chinese servant for her mother.

We know there are some rich Chinese but we don't think about them very much. We don't know where they live, or how, and we don't really care. Sometimes we see very elegant Chinese ladies stepping out of automobiles in their slick gowns, often carrying furs, but to us this is an anomaly. More common in our world and much more believable are the beggars we meet every day on our way to school. We sometimes throw them coppers. There is the dwarf with his large head and sad eyes. He holds out a small grubby hand, the palm engrained with dirt. Then there is the head-banger. He sits on the sidewalk, cross-legged, and periodically cries out in a loud voice at the same time throwing himself forward and crashing his forehead against the cement. His forehead is thickly padded, but nonetheless the effect is stunning. We hurry by him and by the man with elephantiasis who is brought every morning by his relatives and left with his huge dark leg exposed to the hip. The toes are black. They make me feel like throwing up. Yet I look. We both look and shudder. Our favourite is a little girl with long, greasy hair and a charming grin. She turns up in her sad rags, and we always give her something. Sometimes Mother gives me food for her, leftovers from our meals. Once mother gave her one of my old sweaters, and after that every time we met her she would pull the red sleeve of my sweater out from under her rags to show me she was wearing it.

These are the real Chinese, and so is the woman in the tuck shop on the corner who pulls candy out of her jars and wraps it in newspaper, licking her fingers after each transaction. She is a real Chinese, and so is the compradore in the grocery shop on the corner who is so quick on his abacus, and the rickshaw coolies who sit huddled in their rags in the winter waiting for a fare, and who smell so pungently in the hot summers. Chinese dentists and letter-writers set up shop on the sidewalk against a handy wall. The dentists put out their instruments on a grubby table and wait for customers. The letter-writers sit behind their tables with their paper and brushes and bottles of ink servicing those who cannot read or write but who wish to send letters or to have letters read to them.

At this school, as at my old school, no Chinese girls are admitted. Eurasians are allowed only if the father is white. Olga and I accept this easily. We give very little thought to social distinctions, but we are sometimes bothered by the attitude of the English girls in our class. Most English girls attend the exclusive Cathedral School, but we have a few as our classmates. These girls keep apart and have their own little clique. We are never invited to their homes. Even though they do not shine academically, nor excel at sports, yet they give the impression of being superior. "They don't have to be especially good at anything," an Armenian girl explains to us, "they just have to be British." I wonder about that. Are some nationalities just naturally better than others?

As time passes my friendship with Olga deepens. We spend weekends together, we go to movies and fall in love with Errol Flynn and Cary Grant. We are both avid readers and consume, without discrimination, both schoolgirl potboilers and timeless classics. Tennis becomes a craze. Olga excels at it, becomes junior school champion, I win academic awards.

In the long hot summers we play games or visit the Jessfield Park. In the zoo the monkey house is repulsively odiferous and the donkey eats paper bags. We buy Hazelwood icecream bars checking out the bonus letters for a free bar while the city steams around us and the cicadas saw away in the tree tops. My father, covered with prickly heat, mounts to the roof garden and scans the metallic sky for a cloud on the horizon that might spell a typhoon, and drops bits of paper down into the lane to see if there is any hope-giving breeze. The bits of paper flutter straight down.

My sister and her husband take us for drives in the countryside and sometimes on a ferry ride down the Whangpoo River, almost to the mouth of the Yangtsze. Once in a while I get an exciting whiff of a rare salty flavour that I know is the China Sea but the ferry never goes far enough for us actually to see it. Once Olga and I see a dead body floating down the river.

Olga tells me that she and her parents always spend two weeks in Tsingtao, a popular resort in the north. The mention of a vacation is like a thorn pressed into my heart. Everyone I know goes on vacations except my parents and me. My mother feels vacations are a waste of money. To escape the heat for a brief period only makes it that much worse when you return, she says, and Father could never get the time off anyway. She's probably right, but my heart bleeds from that thorn. How I long for climes unknown, for seas and mountains and the romance of travel, but it seems as if this is never to be.

In the fall we buy hot roasted chestnuts and eat them on the way to school. Every day we pass a residence called The Marble Hall. It is very grand, and set in extensive, lushly landscaped grounds. The estate is surrounded by a wall and we can only peek in at the gates. We wonder who owns it.

One day, as we are passing by the Marble Hall, Olga tells me that she's found out who the owner is. He's a Jew.

"A Jew," I repeat stupidly, failing to clue in to the significance of her statement.

A Jew, Olga reiterates. That's why he's so rich. The Jews are all rich. And they're trouble-makers. They started the revolution in Russia, she tells me.

I don't think she's quite right. Louba wasn't rich. But her words ring a bell. I have heard them before, and at my Aunt Lena's house. The Jews and the Bolsheviks. They started the revolution. They caused the fall of the Tsar's empire.

I have no argument to offer, nor do I look for any. It seems reasonable enough. *Someone* must have started the revolution. Certainly "Bolshevik" has been a dirty word ever since I can remember. I have a fearful picture of a Bolshevik in my mind, someone half man and half beast, dressed in rags and carrying a knife in his teeth. Bolsheviks threatened the lives of Aunt Lena and my doctor uncle. Bolsheviks dispossessed my parents and drove the White Russians from their rightful home. Bolshevik and evil are synonymous in my mind.

And the Jews. I remember May Davenport and how she

too had warned me against the Jews.

At home I ask my father about them. "Did they really start the revolution?" I ask. As always he's happy to have a discussion. I cannot give an exact rendering of our talk but its every nuance has remained with me through the years.

"Some people think so," my father says.

"Why?" I ask.

My father settles down in his chair and lights a cigarette. "It stemmed from Karl Marx," he says. "I think we read about him."

"Yes, we did," I say, "but tell me again."

"He was a political philosopher and he came from a family of Jewish rabbis."

I roll back my memory screen. "But I'm sure you said they were Lutherans."

"*Baptized* Lutherans. His father had them all baptized, some say to save his career in Lutheran Prussia. Karl Marx and his friend Friedrich Engels wrote and published a pamphlet called The Communist Manifesto."

"I remember," I say eagerly. "It was something to do with the working people, wasn't it?"

"Yes, it called for all the workers of the world to unite and to stand up for their rights. It became the Bible of revolutionaries everywhere."

"Then a Jew *was* responsible for the idea in the first place."

"Marx was born a Jew but he rejected Judaism. The founder of Christianity was also a Jew. Would you call Christianity a Jewish plot?" My father smiles.

I shrug this off. 'Well, are they bad people?"

"No *people* are bad," my father says. "There are good and bad individuals in every group, Jews and Russians alike, and usually no-one is wholly good or bad. Except for us Estonians of course," he adds, with that same enigmatic smile. "We're all perfect."

I bypass the gentle joke. "Who did start the revolution

then?" I ask.

"When people are oppressed for too long something gives way. The revolution had been creeping up on the Russians for a long time. It was inevitable the way things were."

"Don't you hate them?" I ask, "the people who caused the revolution, who made you lose everything?"

My fathers butts out his cigarette. He shakes his head. "In a way we may have been to blame ourselves," he says. "On the whole we ignored the suffering of the poor. It was bound to happen. But Russia's so huge and we weren't important enough to have much say anyway. It's pointless to be angry now. Still, I'm sad, of course. I wish I could have given you a better life." He gives me a little hug.

I begin to think about the Jews and about all the other nationalities. The British are snobby, the Chinese not quite people, the Jews are suspect, the Reds and Bolsheviks out and out evil according to their victims. It is my first true recognition of the fact that everyone is different, that we aren't all one happy family, that there is wariness and often outright hostility floating in the air around me. Now I remember having heard the Japanese described as not trustworthy, did they not attack Vladivostok while everyone slept, and appropriate Dairen and and Port Arthur? And only recently they occupied Manchuria. And the Scottish people are tight with their money, there are always jokes about them, and the Americans are showoffs, and the Sikhs quick with their truncheons on the backs of hapless rickshaw coolies.

How is it that the distinguishing characteristics of these differing people are all unpleasant? Why do we spotlight only unpleasant characteristics? I sit next to an Indian girl in class, from a Sikh family, and she is gravely considerate. She is the only one who has ever congratulated me on my good grades. I have met her father and he is gracious, a fine gentleman in his elegant turban. I'm sure he would never take a truncheon to anyone.

Chapter Eleven

Racial antagonisms were not alone in creating confusion in my early life. Religion, too, took a hand. My Lutheran parents, although respecting the church, attended it only on Christmas Eve. My sister had adopted the Anglican church. My cousin Nina was a Russian Orthodox.

My father did not like Catholics, my Aunt Lena did not like Jews and everybody without exception around me despised the pagan religion of the Chinese in whose country they had settled. I grew up with the firm notion that Buddhist temples had a pall of evil over them, and that the Chinese pantheon of gods, including such beneficent deities as the Goddess of Mercy and the Kitchen God, were pernicious fairytales better abandoned in favour of our own Christian beliefs. Our own belief in a God-man born of a virgin, who was crucified, died, was buried and then rose from the dead to ascend to the skies and to live there forever with his Father, did not seem improbable to me when I was little. It did not occur to me that it, too, bore all the trademarks of a myth, a beautiful and sad legend of betrayal and death with a tacked-on happy ending born of wishful thinking. I took it all on faith and believed easily and mindlessly.

My sister nurtured my belief by her own unswerving loyalty to Christian principles and from the direction of my cousin Nina and her parents blew a wind of enormous religious fervour. My doctor uncle was dedicated to the Russian Orthodox faith, Aunt Lena had converted to orthodoxy when she had married him and Nina, totally immersed in that faith, did not question it.

An atmosphere of staunch religiosity pervaded Nina's home. Every religious festival was observed and there was an icon in a corner of each room with its little oil lamp, the holy lampada, burning day and night. The icons fascinated me. They were sombre and beautiful, with their glowing lampadas throwing mysterious shadows, and emanating a sense of alien sacredness that left me feeling excluded and vaguely inferior. We had nothing like that in our Protestant household to indicate the presence of God in our home. My father said that icons could lead to idolatry, that the simpler Russians believed in the icons themselves rather than in the deity they represented. But he never voiced this opinion in Nina's home.

I believed my father but when I was at Nina's house I felt differently. Her home was frequented by the deacons and the archimandrites of the Orthodox Church. In addition to his devoutness, the doctor was a generous financial supporter of the church, and the priests appreciated this, and also the unstinting medical assistance he rendered to the penurious White Russians free of charge. They reciprocated in the only way they could, by offering him their friendship and their blessings, although my Aunt Lida, newly arrived from the Soviet Union and still a Lutheran, allowed her skepticism to escape once in a while, and filled my young mind with doubts about the sincerity of the priests.

In addition to Aunt Lida's skepticism, the Russian priests themselves made me uncomfortable. It was obvious to me, even at that age, that they regarded me as a lost soul. I was afraid of them, of their occult ambience. They moved slowly, their black robes billowing around them. Great silver crosses swung on their chests, like menacing charms. The smell of incense clung to them. Their long hair marked them as holy men. On special occasions, when the archimandrite came to bless the house and conduct a small private ceremony, he wore an elaborate head-dress. He lifted his voice in sonorous chants. It was theatrical and he was certainly more impressive than the Protestant ministers who, upon their rare house visits, differed from laymen only in regard to their back-to-front collars.

The priests fostered the hopes of the White Russians for a counter revolution. The destruction of the Orthodox Church was synonymous with the destruction of Mother Russia. Their livelihood had been snatched away from them. The terror of destitution faced them. There was no-one to turn to in the alien country to which they had come, social assistance was unheard of, they had no skills. Their plight was pitiable. Anyone like my uncle who was willing to subsidize the church was understandably a literal Godsend. And he, for his part, must have felt that the church was a reliable coagulant. It provided a focal point for the White Russian community, it nurtured the spirit of Holy Russia.

Much as I loved my orthodox relatives, close as I had become to my friend Olga, a discomfort crept into my relationship with them, setting up an unhappy dichotomy in my mind. The majority of the White Russians in Shanghai were poor, they had been the losers in the civil war, and even though the world condemned the winners, it is not easy for a loser to re-establish himself in the eyes of the world or in his own. Most White Russians spoke poor English and held menial jobs. They were considered second-class citizens. Prostitutes were Chinese or White Russian girls. Among my British acquaintances at my Anglican Sunday School, I never mentioned my White Russian connections. I made sure that the girls at school knew that I was *Estonian,* not Russian. I don't think this made the slightest difference to any of them, nor did any one of them have the faintest notion where or what Estonia was, but it pleased me to have this refuge. I was glad both my father and sister spoke good English. I was embarrassed by my mother who did not. The shallowness of this attitude was not apparent to my teen mind.

Religion was the hub around which each community revolved, and the root of societal divisions. Within the social life of the city the members of the different communities seldom mixed. Although we resented the reserve of the British girls, they were probably as much victims of circumstance as any of the rest of us, trapped by their own circle, their own mores. It takes unusual courage and convictions to step out of prescribed limits. We all tend to fall into comfortable patterns.

I had become accustomed to the austere Cathedral with its polished pews and the faces of the apostles staring down at me from the windows in stained-glass neutrality. The Dean, no less pompous than the Russian priests, was nonetheless respected in his own country, unlike the priests who had been driven out of theirs. He was there by his own choice, paid well, able to live in style. Contrary to the devastation in Russia the British Empire was a dominant entity. I was favoured by the ministers at the Cathedral because I could recite all those texts. It was gratifying to be top-rated by people who lived in gracious homes and drove expensive cars, but in my heart I knew I did not truly belong in that rarefied atmosphere. I was an extremely confused young person. My loyalties were being sadly strained.

So it was not surprising that in my fourteenth year I suddenly lost my belief in God.

One night I woke up to a sense of total vacuity. It may have been triggered by some adult conversation I had overheard, perhaps by my father's love of the philosophers, so many of an atheistic bent, but most probably it was the logical result of the confusion that had been eating away at my mind. I was in the grip of panic, convinced that there was no presence at all, loving or otherwise, in the universe around me. There was no evidence of any kind of God. He did not speak to us. The prophets might well have been dreaming, there was nothing to prove they had heard God's voice. *I* had never heard it. I plunged into a depth of aloneness all the more devastating for being so new. The universe was huge and empty. It was absurd to imagine anyone out there in the abysses of space, never mind anyone who gave a fig for me. I lay in bed and sweated.

I thought of the death of Jesus and the resurrection. How could anyone rise from the dead? What if you were eaten by lions in Africa? How could you rise incorruptible then? That's what it said—that we would be raised incorruptible. Was it only our souls that would be resurrected? What did we know of souls?

The doubts came tumbling over each other, attacking me like demons with stilettos. And I suddenly thought that perhaps that's just what it was. It was the devil tempting me away from belief in God. Just as he had tempted Jesus!

I began to pray, my words tumbling out as fast as the doubts came pouring in. I used the words I had heard in church. I prayed for belief, for help against the devil. I prayed to Jesus, I prayed to God. It was like a chant, a mantra, and under its hypnotic spell I fell asleep. But when I woke in the morning I knew that the prayers had not helped. They had lulled me to sleep but my doubts were still there. True, the universe did not look as threatening in the cheerful light of morning, with Maria Mikhailovna scolding Ledda, and Ah Foh clanking dishes in the kitchen, but in a strangely adult way I remember thinking that the sun and the morning were the illusions, and the real thing was the terror that lay at the heart of life, the terror of the darkness and the void. It was this terror I would have to learn to accommodate in order to survive.

I was still going to Sunday School, but suddenly after that night, I quit. My mother was vaguely disturbed, but I told her I was too old for Sunday School. She shrugged. My father didn't say anything. I had only another year to go before my confirmation.

I announced that I didn't want to be confirmed.

I could see they were shocked, though there was no significant sign of their displeasure, but my father said it was better to be confirmed, to belong to a church.

I said I didn't believe in God.

My father replied that not everyone actually *believed* in God. We all hoped He existed and was just and loving.

"Just and loving!" I cried, "with so much misery in the

world? And how do we know He's there at all? He never speaks to us."

My father reminded me that some people felt He did. He also pointed out that we knew so very little and the universe was so very vast, we could only speculate. It wasn't up to us to make judgments.

His words, so wise had I stopped to ponder all their possible ramifications, only served to exasperate me. Perhaps we were insignificant but our terror was enormous. My terror had filled the whole night, it had filled the universe.

My parents did not press anything, but the wheels began to turn, possibly on the instigation of my sister. A short time after I had made my announcement, the Reverend Ottewell came to call on me.

The Reverend Ottewell was a remarkable man. He was subordinate to the Dean of the Cathedral, who was distantly gracious and imposing, but who did not mix very much with the hoi polloi. I stood in awe of the Dean. He was a large man with an impressive voice. In the Cathedral, clad in his black and white vestments highlighted by scarlet, he was a commanding figure indeed. I never spoke to him. I saw him in church every Sunday and sometimes at Sunday School sessions, when, even though plainly dressed in a black suit with a clerical collar, he still compelled us with his lordly presence. I also saw him every year at the annual picnic and prize-giving at which I invariably received a prize for my mindless spouting of Biblical texts. These joyful occasions took place on the estate of one of the wealthier families in the city. They were notable for the feasts, presented on long tables covered with white linen and set out on immaculate lawns, of sandwiches, buns, cakes and lemonade, and were arranged by hostesses who held elevated positions on the social ladder. I was left with a delightful and indelible impression of spacious grounds, wide beds of gay flowers, the brilliant light of the Shanghai summers and the distinction of being an annual prize winner. At these functions, year after year, the Dean handed out the prizes, beaming benevolently but remotely upon each recipient, rather like the noonday sun of the creator he represented. He gave no impression of knowing any child personally, or ever wanting to.

But the Reverend Ottewell was quite different. He mingled with the fold. He did not only speak about the lambs of God, he came among them, undismayed by their earthiness, by the dirt on their woolly coats. He shared his love and his concern in a variety of tangible ways, by visiting the sick, by listening to people's worries, by arranging and attending discussion groups for young adults. Instead of patting children on the head, he talked to them.

I had not counted on having to face the Reverend Ottewell.

He came without warning. I became flustered. I was messy, dressed in old, unflattering clothes. A girlish vanity was at work. I had no idea why he was calling.

He talked to me in the dining-room and I wished our home were more like the elegant homes of his English parishioners. I thought of the open cement garbage containers at the entrance to each row of houses that he had passed on his way into the complex and writhed inwardly with embarrassment. But he showed no interest in our surroundings. He had heard, he said, that I wanted to leave Sunday School, that there seemed to be some question about my confirmation.

To my surprise I found myself correcting him. I said there was no *question.* I *didn't want* to be confirmed.

He asked me to tell him why.

I was tongue-tied. How could I tell this good man of God that I didn't believe in his God any more? That I had discovered that the universe, far from being filled with the loving presence of a heavenly Father, was in fact a mind-boggling void. That prayer didn't help a whit.

He suggested, very gently, that perhaps I felt too old for

Sunday School.

I seized the straw. "Yes, I do feel that," I said.

He asked me if I realized that I was their best student? He would be sorry to lose me.

Flattery? No. It was the truth. At least the one who could memorize best.

Was I having doubts about religion, perhaps?

I was surprised. How did he know? Could he read my mind? My nervousness increased.

He told me that there was nothing wrong with that. He assured me that everyone had doubts from time to time.

I stared at him. Doubts? He? This man who joined the Dean Sunday after Sunday in sonorous prayers addressed to the Lord, who spoke to us children about the love of God and Jesus, about the heaven where we were headed to live forever in bliss in the mansions Jesus had prepared for us?

Doubts?

He nodded slowly. It was true, he told me. That was the reason why I should stay with them—because we could all help one another. Soon I would be old enough to join in the discussion groups he held in the church. The church, he went on, was only a symbol of what we all felt inside. He begged me not to throw it all away, to give it a bit more time.

I had little power to resist this soft-spoken, reasonable man. His persuasiveness wrapped around me like the loving presence of the God I had just lost. Perhaps he was right. Although fourteen seemed like a truly great age, perhaps it was too early to make a decision.

I had little power, but I had some. I did not promise him anything. I said I would think about it. In my own mind I doubted very much that I would come round to his way of thinking but I could not flatly refuse him. He seemed satisfied. I was glad when he left. When his penetrating presence had gone from the house I felt free, I felt courageous. I decided I would defy him. But that evening an event occurred that shook me to the very depths of my fourteen-year-old psyche.

At about nine o'clock I was lying in bed, reading. At this time the house was usually very quiet. The grownups were downstairs in the dining-room, three flights of stairs away, having a last cup of tea, chatting about the events of the day. I could hear them only faintly and soon I lost all awareness of them in the fascinating story unfolding before me between the pages of my book. My door was closed.

Suddenly I heard a thump against my door. I looked up, as yet without alarm. There was another thump, and then there was a series of groans. They did not sound human. My heart tightened. The thump was repeated and there was the sound as of something, or someone gasping for breath, choking. At this I was catapulted into action. I leaped out of bed and threw open my door.

On the small landing outside my room, between the bathroom door and the head of the stairs, lay Ledda. She lay on her side, her legs stretched out unnaturally. She was shuddering violently, and she appeared to be choking. Her eyes were rolled back, her mouth slightly opened. Foam speckled with blood was escaping from her mouth. She gasped for breath between the convulsions, drawing in air with a rasping sound.

I screamed. The tea-drinkers downstairs heard me and came rushing up. At the sight of Ledda they were shocked for a brief moment into immobility. My father said to me, "Go into your room and shut the door."

Maria Mikhailovna said, "I'll get the vet." Her face was pale, large eyes staring, unable to let go of the sight of the suffering animal. She hurried downstairs, still looking back. I went into my room and shut the door part way, but I couldn't shut Ledda out of my life. My father repeated his injunction. His voice conveyed to me the intensity of his anxiety and I knew I must obey. I closed the door and huddled against the cold metal headrail of my bed.

Ledda continued to thump and gasp. The grownups talked in low, frightened voices. I could hear Ah Foh adding his bit to the subdued consternation. Maria Mikhailovna asked him what Ledda had been eating. In his obscure English he was trying to justify anything he may have fed the dog during the day. Suddenly there was silence. My heart closed against the meaning of that silence, but its message was clear. I cried out and sprang to the door to look out again. My father repeated his injunction to keep the door shut but I was staring at Ledda, lying stretched out stiff and still.

The vet arrived, too late. He couldn't have helped in any case. His surmise was that Ledda had been poisoned.

I went back to bed, pulling the blankets around me. I was shivering though the house was warm. There were more phonecalls. After quite some time during which I fell into a light, exhausted doze, I was awakened by strange voices and footsteps. There were thumping sounds outside my door, a burden being dragged. I knew what was happening. After the visitants had gone downstairs with their fearful load, I heard Ah Foh come upstairs, clanking with his mop and bucket. He spent a lot of time washing the landing. I heard Mother and Maria Mikhailovna giving him instructions. A smell of disinfectant filtered in. After this my door opened and my mother looked in. Seeing that I was not asleep she came and sat beside me on my bed.

I clung to her. She hugged me silently for a long time.

The next day we learned from the vet that our Ledda had been poisoned with strychnine-laced meat. The police came and found remnants of it in our little yard. Someone had thrown it over the fence. They told us that Ledda was not the first victim, that someone had been poisoning Great Danes. Their motive was unexplained. It could have been something to do with rival breeders, the police said.

But I knew better. I knew it had to do with my revolt against the church. Against God. It was my punishment.

No-one was as deeply affected by Ledda's death as I was. Maria Mikhailovna shook her head and looked sad, but I was sure she was not suffering as I was. "It was only a dog," my Uncle Ernest said. "We can get another."

Ledda was not only a dog. Ledda was my friend and companion. She understood everything I said, intuited when I was sad and when I was glad. She waited for me when I got home from school and overwhelmed me with affection. I had been punished. And it was probably only the start of my punishment. If I didn't come to my senses there might be worse to come. Perhaps my fears about losing my mother would materialize. I was afraid of the God in whom I no longer believed.

The next day I told my parents that I had reconsidered. I would be confirmed next year. I would go to the Reverend Ottewell's classes.

The Reverend Ottewell smiled his quiet smile. I was redirected to the path of Christianity.

Chapter Twelve

Temporarily I laid aside my doubts. I knew I had pleased the people I loved best. That I had displeased the burgeoning entity within myself gave me a sense of vague discomfort, but my superstitious fear of divine displeasure was too great to allow that discomfort precedence. I ignored it but it did not dissipate. It remained and steadily ate away at the basic structure of those beliefs that had been inculcated into my subconscious throughout my childhood, but of this I was as yet unaware.

It wasn't difficult to disregard the discomfort. I had entered an exciting stage of my life. I was immersed in school activities, in classroom honours and class projects. I sailed through tests and exams on the wings of my Crazy-glue memory. Cast in the role of Puck in *A Midsummer-Night's Dream* I discovered I had a flair for the stage. Aided no doubt by the encouraging roominess of the new bed, I began to grow, relieving my mother of the fear that I would be arrested for life at four feet six. Olga and I went tennis-mad. She outdid her own brilliant performance of the previous year and won the Senior championship, and together we won the doubles. The following year I was Petruchio in *The Taming of the Shrew*. The play made local history, it was written up in the foremost paper with flattering reference to my efforts amd carried a photograph of the cast. Dreams of a great future on the Shakespearian stage floated through my foolish mind.

But alas, these glories met with little enthusiasm at home. I was praised, but perfunctorily. Our home life was in the throes of a crisis that I in my self-absorption had entirely failed to register.

The first sign of the impending crisis was the advent of Chief. Chief was a Boston bull pup. Maria Mikhailovna brought him home to console herself for the loss of Ledda. Chief was saucy and rambunctious and I didn't like him very much. He had baleful eyes. He snarled and snapped and ate everything in sight. My mother launched a strong protest and Maria Mikhailovna agreed to keep him shut up in her bedroom during the hours she and Uncle Ernest were away at their jobs. Chief fouled the room, which was newly spread with newspapers every morning and systematically chewed through the furnishings. Cushions, mats, blankets, upholstery, all went. Corners of the elegant dresser and wardrobe and the legs of chairs were gnawed through by his pernicious teeth and the contents of drawers left open accidentally, were summarily masticated. Lamps were pulled down and shades torn apart. Before they left in the morning, Uncle Ernest and Maria Mikhailovna were obliged to strip the bed and stand the mattress up on end behind the headboard. The one soft armchair that remained had been turned over to Chief and it was worried to shreds, the stuffing hung out, the springs, released from their mooring, stood up in drunken rows. The carpet, or what was left of it, had long been removed and the floor under the newspapers was indelibly stained. The stench was formidable even though the windows were left open all day long.

Maria Mikhailovna assured my appalled mother that once Chief was past the puppy stage he would change. My mother waited. Chief did not change. He simply grew larger, snappier and more rambunctious when he was released from his prison, pulverizing everything in sight with greater ferocity and more malice than ever.

At the same time during this period, I would hear what I dreaded more than anything else, the sound of quarrelling. There were raised voices, sobbing, the slamming of doors. Over and over again I would hear my Uncle Ernest leave the house, my mother expostulate with Maria Mikhailovna, my Uncle Ernest return and then my father's voice, full of stress, urging reconciliation. All this came to me muffled, through closed doors, so that I never heard the actual burden of the rows and therefore presumed that they were to do with the awful Chief. For a long time I had no idea of their true nature, and of its gravity.

Perhaps I did not want to know. That there was conflict among my relatives was a matter of great potential embarrassment to me. I was afraid one of those scenes might erupt when Olga was visiting me. And so during the periods of truce I put them entirely out of my mind and reverted to my own fascinating pastimes, hoping that they would never recur.

But recur they did. It was gradually borne in upon me that the scenes had nothing to do with Chief, that their origin lay in something quite different, of which Chief was only symptomatic. Slowly and unwillingly I understood that Maria Mikhailovna, the kindest and most generous of women, suffered from a woeful malaise. This malaise was an unreasoning possessiveness.

Maria Mikhailovna appeared to be showing a side of her nature that had been concealed earlier from all but the penetrating assessment of Aunt Lena who had perhaps discovered the reason for her divorce and feared for Uncle Ernest's happiness. A divorcée was a potential disaster. What had happened once could happen again.

Maria Mikhailovna was passionately resentful of anyone with whom Uncle Ernest spent any amount of time, even of his own sisters. This did sound unreasonable, but I found it hard to fault the woman who had been so good to me. Her unhappiness weighed upon me. *Could* Uncle Ernest be to blame in some way? I had no way of knowing. The distress of the adults around me loomed huge and unresolvable and filled my days with gloom. Now when I walked into the house at Victory Terrace I would pause at the foot of the stairs, towering above me full of foreboding, and wait for the sounds I dreaded to hear. In those moments of helplessness my heart hardened against those who burdened me with their conflicts. Compassion was fast slipping away.

It was only in later years, as the tragedy developed, that I began to wonder whether the distrust the family harboured at the start of the romance had become a self-fulfilling prophecy. Hostility had bred insecurity in its victim and this had turned into paranoia proving that the family had been right, that the marriage should never have taken place. Maria Mikhailovna must have known that her acceptance into the family had been only on a superficial level—no-one in the family had ever been moved to call her Maria, she was addressed formally as Maria Mikhailovna to her last day.

I needed an escape from the gloom that closed in upon me whenever I entered our Victory Terrace home and fortunately a new vista opened before me that fall. I had started to take the classes in preparation for my confirmation in the

Anglican Church, and an interesting new species of animal life had swum into my ken. Prior to this the only boy I had ever spoken to had been Sonnyboy on Sun Avenue and he had turned out to be a big disappointment! But here were these creatures, dressed in grey flannels and purple jackets, seated in a row in such close proximity I could have reached out and touched them, though that thought stopped the very flow of blood in my veins. I felt at a disadvantage to the girls around me. They were all British, as were the boys, and most of them were from the posh Cathedral School. Many of them knew the boys, some were related. Among them I was an anomaly. None of them ever knew the prescribed lessons as I did, but that didn't matter, as my classmate had said, they only had to be British.

Still, it was exciting. I could taste privilege on my tongue, and it was a wonderful taste. One or two of the girls were friendly and my hopes rose. Perhaps in time they might even accept me as one of themselves, although I knew full well I could never invite them to my home with the garbage containers outside and the dissensions within.

In the spring of the following year Chief suddenly died. He had chewed through his last stick of furniture. My mother tried to appear sympathetic but failed. She was so happy to be rid of the beast that she took me to the Basket Fair and in a moment of joyful impulse-buying chose a fine bamboo shelf for my books replacing the table that had been damaged by the storm in Sun Avenue. But her jubilation was short-lived.

One day I came home from church bearing good news. I had passed all my tests at the top of the confirmation class. I was elated. I thought everyone else would be too.

I found the family in the dining-room. Maria Mikhailovna was seated in a corner armchair and at her feet in a basket were two of the most adorable pups I had ever seen. They were Alsatians. My Uncle Ernest was by the French windows, his back to the room. My father perched on the edge of a chair by the arcola, lighting a cigarette with shaking hands. And my mother was standing by the table, holding onto the back of a chair. It was my mother's face that held me riveted.

A bright pink glowed high on her cheeks. There was a peculiar twist to her mouth. Her hands worked up and down the back of the chair. No-one paid the slightest attention to my entry.

My mother said, "You must either get rid of those dogs or find somewhere else to live."

I had never heard my mother speak so bluntly, nor had I ever heard a tone like that in her voice.

"Surely you are being unreasonable," Maria Mikhailovna said. "They're such darlings." She looked around at us out of hurt brown eyes—the eyes I had seen so often brim over with goodwill upon presenting me with some unwarranted gift.

"Those darlings will grow up to be monsters like your precious Chief," my mother said in that new raised voice.

"Manichka," my father murmured soothingly, using his fond name for her, "please don't excite yourself."

"Then why don't *you* say something," she cried, lashing out at my father's mild, non-aggressive nature. "You never say anything. You agree to everything and then *I* have to suffer." He grimaced in pain and she swung back to the hapless Maria Mikhailovna. "I'm sick to death of you and your quarrels and your stupid dogs! Either those dogs go or you do!"

My father, after a few nervous puffs, put down his cigarette and rose to stand behind my mother, holding her arms with his hands as if to prevent her from blowing apart. Maria Mikhailovna picked up the basket with the pups and left the room. And Uncle Ernest, with a strange little gurgle, succumbed to an anxiety attack.

His face became drawn, he gasped and wheezed, he clutched his chest. He collapsed in the vacated easy chair.

"Should we call the doctor?" asked my father shakily.

"Of course not," my mother snapped. "He'll get over it. Go and get the valerian drops," she said to me sharply. Was she remembering her own attack and how it had been minimized?

I raced up the five flights of stairs to her room and flew down again, taking three steps at each leap, clutching the bottle of drops. My mother administered the medication to my uncle. Then she took a few drops herself. She sank down into a chair, panting. "Mama," I said, grasping her arm, terrified in case she should suddenly take leave of this life, "Mama, don't you want to hear about my tests?"

"Don't bother me now," she said, waving me aside peremptorily.

"Later, darling, later," my father said, nudging me away.

I ran out of the room, raced up the stairs again to my own bedroom and threw myself down on my bed. For the first time there percolated through my mind the intimation of an incredible possibility—that I might not be the centre of the universe, even in my parents' books. How could they have dismissed me so unfeelingly?

Soon after this Uncle Ernest and Maria Mikhailovna moved out. Upon parting my father said to Uncle Ernest that Maria Mikhailovna was ill, that she should see a doctor. Uncle Ernest dismissed this idea, but years later I was to recall my father's chilling perspicacity.

Upon the departure of my relatives, hope briefly surfaced that we too might leave Victory Terrace, but to my deep humiliation a "Room to Let" sign went up on our door. To live with relatives was bad enough, but to have to rent a room was degradation itself. It put a final cap on any hope I may have had of ever being recognized as an equal by my British acquaintances.

It was the sitting-room on the second floor that my mother let. She moved me into the top bedroom, and in an unprecedented move she settled my father by himself in my room and took the room that had been Uncle Ernest's for herself. She announced that she could no longer sleep in the same room as my father. He snored and he smoked, and she'd had enough of it. He wanted the windows closed, and she wanted them open.

The separation of my parents into different rooms meant little to me. I was extremely naïve and had no knowledge whatsoever of sex. With my head stuffed full of facts, Biblican texts and endless passages from tedious poets, my curiosity about methods of procreation was nil. Perhaps it was not that surprising or unusual in those days. No-one ever mentioned sex at home or in any of the homes I visited. There was no television and the books I read were schoolgirl stories, mysteries, fantasies and innocent romances. Through my talks with my father, I had a vague understanding of the philosophers, but these thinkers were concerned with such subjects as the origin of all life, man's place in the universe, the relationship of good to evil and the existence or non-existence of God. Procreation was not a great matter to them, it was no mystery. The rumblings of Freud were certainly not a subject for dinner-time conversation nor would my father have ever dreamt of expounding on the subject of sex to me—had he unwisely done so on one of his expansive evenings after a glass or two of vodka my mother would have barred him from her favour for days. Once when I was older and asked my mother in a moment of uncharacteristic curiosity as to what *marriage* actually entailed, she told me that when I found a husband he would enlighten me.

As far as love was concerned, I figured I knew all about that, hadn't I myself fallen in love with Vickery and with Sonnyboy, and with Errol Flynn and Cary Grant? But it had never occurred to me to wonder what the logical conclusions of those excitations could be. I thought the highpoint of love was a kiss and a wedding. I had never for one moment ever imagined anyone engaged in anything like the sexual act, least of all my parents. I didn't know there was a sexual act.

How I thought I came into the world I have no idea.

So the sleeping arrangements of my parents caused me no alarm and in fact no alarm was called for because that was as far as the matter went. My parents remained as friendly and warm and concerned about one another as they had ever been. Typically, what was of far greater consequence to me was the fact that I could now have the room that adjoined the roof garden with its accompanying sizeable landing for my very own. Though it by no means wiped out the indignity of the "Room to Let" sign, having the top of the house to myself was a considerable consolation. I moved in with my books and my Bible and my triangular blue vase arranged on the new bamboo shelf.

My mother, possibly on a wave of guilt for her behaviour to me on the day of the quarrel, now plunged with great fervour into plans for my confirmation. The sewing-machine went into action again and she and Aunt Lida cut and stitched and whirled until a beautiful white dress for the occasion emerged from under their deft hands. In the warmth of this attention, the momentary suspicion that I was not the centre of the universe melted away and I, too, entered into the preparations with enthusiasm.

I scrutinized myself in the mirror. My face was heart-shaped, which was singular, and my eyes, though a fairly agreeable greenish-blue, were far too alert for allure, a bit like the new traffic lights on our street. I practised gazing out from under lowered lids to achieve a sultry effect, with no success. My hair was still blond, but it was losing the platinum tones once admired by the banished Maria Mikhailovna. Fine and thick, it curled easily if I took some trouble with it, which I very seldom did, so it usually hung loose and looked ratty. I had a curious tiptilted nose and dimples that were embarrassing. My scrutiny was not encouraging. I saw nothing that might bring the mysterious opposite sex in a rush to my feet.

Still, that was all I had to work with, and in a spurt of zeal

I made a special effort. The night before the great day I curled my hair by rolling strands round a pencil and fastening them with bobby pins. The next morning my hair looked strangely fuzzy and caused some wonder in the household. When I was dressed, I powdered my face, but when I begged my mother for rouge she squashed the idea at once. A few of the girls were using lipstick, but there was not the remotest hope of that for me. I bit my lips to make them red. They became sore and chapped.

The service was solemn but also festive. The Cathedral was decorated with white flowers, the Dean and the Reverend Ottewell had on their grandest robes and the whole choir was present. The soloist sang "Oh for the Wings of a Dove." She was known for this musical gem and sang it often. I admired her clear, floating voice. I myself couldn't sing at all.

The girls were all dressed in white, the boys in dark suits, and they sat on opposite sides of the aisle. I stole glances at the boys, blushing and swiftly turning away when I caught their equally curious eyes. An extraordinary excitement filled me. I perspired and my face powder mixed with my sweat and turned into tiny balls that stuck humiliatingly to my skin.

Sonorously and relentlessly the service moved forward. We were asked questions and we answered them. We knelt and murmured prayers and sang. The Dean spoke in his deep, resonant voice, the choir intoned melodiously. We moved toward the altar rail for our first communion. We went back to our seats. There was more singing, then a final blessing from the Dean. We were confirmed. We were now true members of the church.

And upon this pronouncement I was suddenly overcome by guilt. I knew that the persuasions of the Reverend Ottewell, the grave overview of my parents and the example of my friends had had no effect whatsoever on the unbelief that had wedged itself tightly somewhere between my ribs.

The Certificate of Confirmation, tied with a red ribbon, dampened in my sweaty hands. I knew myself for a true hypocrite.

At home there was a party in my honour. My parents gave me a watch, my Aunt Lena gave me a bracelet of red and white gold interwoven in an intricate design. I had never seen such an elegant bracelet and I was delighted. Maria Mikhailovna and Uncle Ernest had sent a gift of money, they and my mother were not as yet sufficiently reconciled for visiting privileges.

My sister gave me a leather Book of Common Prayer with gold lettering on the cover and gild-edged pages, and she told me that her real gift to me would be a holiday that summer.

I couldn't believe it. A holiday away from Shanghai was what I craved above all things. The shadow of guilt and hypocrisy melted away in the warmth of such a felicitous gift. Despite the niggling voice funnelling up from my heart I assured myself that I must have done the right thing to be this lucky. I consigned my painful ambivalence to the most inaccessible depths of my psyche and concentrated only on present joys. Where would I go? I cried. How? With whom?

Chapter Thirteen

We drive to the docks along our famous Bund, past all the imposing buildings representing business and commerce lining its frontage, with their national flags waving gaily in a rare summer breeze from the river. I am wearing a blue travelling-dress my mother has made me for the trip, a white broad-brimmed hat, socks and new white walking-shoes. I am going to Peitaiho with my doctor uncle, Aunt Lena and Nina on the vacation my sister has arranged. Later we will go to Peking. I am at last old enough to travel without my parents.

Parting from my parents was traumatic. It was the first time I had ever left them. I spent a night in my mother's bed full of lachrymose remorse for agreeing to go, vowing I would never leave her, would cancel the trip. She knew better than to protest. With daybreak my distress vanished.

At the docks, to the chanting of the labouring coolies, the yells of foremen and the rasping of winches, we board a small coastal steamer that will take us to Chinwantao in the north. From Chinwantao we will travel to Peitaiho by train.

As we move out of the mouth of the Yangtsze into the sea, my uncle draws my attention to the colour bar from shore to shore, the water of the delta is a rich, yellowy brown and the sea a deep blue. Once on the sea the ship starts to roll a little. There is a fresh, salty taste to the air. I hold on to the rail savouring ecstasy. My uncle laughs.

My uncle has become a different person. The gravity has slipped off his face. He has an expensive camera slung around his neck and he takes shots of us against the ship's rail. He is a photography buff. At home he has his own dark-room where he develops and prints his pictures. Sometimes, because he is very busy, the prints don't appear for months, but he never takes his films to a developing studio in spite of my Aunt Lena's frequent urgings.

Nina and I share a cabin. She has grown very beautiful and she has lovely clothes. I feel scrawny beside her, all elbows and knees and lank hair, but she is unassuming, deflecting my open admiration with a small laugh. She lets me choose the upper bunk. I have never slept in a bunk.

Just before I drift off I feel a vague and brief anxiety about the tons of water all around us. I also remember that August is the month for typhoons.

I wake to the dazzle of sunlight through the porthole.

Throwing on my clothes, I wake Nina, but she is sleepy and wants to stay in bed. The sea is nothing new to her.

But I run up on deck and am blinded by the splendour of the sun on the water. There is nothing but water in sight, deep and blue and rolling. The horizon heaves slightly. The wind whips through my hair, spirited, smelling of brine, enticing me with mysteries of the fabled China seas.

Nina has dragged herself up for breakfast but still looks sleepy. My uncle surprises me by teasing her. I have never heard him tease anyone before. I have a hearty breakfast and he chuckles at my vast appetite, nodding approval.

Sometime toward noon my uncle calls us to the rail of the ship and shows us the medusas, huge jellyfish that surround the vessel. They hang close to the surface and gleam, changing colours as they shift around in the water. He tells us August is the month for jellyfish and we will have to watch out for them when we swim because they sting. I am repulsed and fascinated by their huge, bloated bodies and long waving tentacles. I remember how I was Perseus and killed the Medusa.

Toward evening we reach Chinwantao and the ship docks. We pack our suitcases, hand them in for unloading and board a small, stuffy train.

Everywhere I look there are hills of coal. Chinwantao is the coal port of the north. My uncle tells me that the anthracite we burn in our arcola comes all the way from the northern mines via Chinwantao. I see coal being loaded into holds of cargo ships. A fine wire mesh covers the train windows and the glass is lightly powdered with coal dust.

Our trip on the train to Peitaiho is short. We are to stay at a boarding-house, something I have never done before.

We rent two bedrooms on the ground floor. A wide verandah runs the length of the house. There is a dining-room at the back where we will have all our meals. I am thrilled at the prospect of "eating out" for three whole weeks. Nina is not roused to the same enthusiasm, she's eaten out often, but she warms to mine, kindly overlooking my lack of sophistication.

We quickly fall into a routine. Every morning after breakfast we set out for the beach. My aunt packs some fruit, which she has carefully disinfected, for a mid-morning snack. We lie on the sand and venture out into the sea. I don't swim well, but the water is sparkling, clear and warm. There are very few people on the beach and no Chinese at all. The sand is a rich yellow and stretches in a crescent for miles. The sea breaks in small cream-topped waves. My aunt has bought us all huge straw hats to guard against the sun.

At noon we start back to our boarding-house for lunch, after which my aunt and uncle disappear into their room for a siesta and Nina and I go to ours. Nina supplies me with candy and we both settle down with our books. I read a story set in the South Pacific about love and longing and atolls and moonlit nights. The heroine has golden eyes. In spite of its entrancing tale, the book soon falls from my hand and I drift off.

We are wakened by a little bell. Mid-afternoon tea is being served on the verandah. We sit at small tables covered with white cloths and a Chinese baker comes around with a basket of cakes and buns. I am allowed to choose whatever I want from the basket. The decision-making is agonizing. Everything looks delectable.

After tea we all go for a long walk. We usually walk to the point at the end of the crescent. Sometimes we walk to the railway station to see the train come in. On the way home we buy candy and Aunt Lena stops at a fruit merchant for peaches and mangoes. Back at the boarding-house she will wash them in potassium permanganate and they will acquire a faintly mauve tint but be safe to eat.

Sometimes before dinner Nina and I hire donkeys for a ride. The donkeys are small and cute and are operated by Chinese "mafoos" or donkey masters. If Nina is feeling tired I go by myself. I ride into the low hills through the woods.

The mafoo walks behind the donkey, prodding him occasionally. My Aunt Lena has no qualms about allowing me to ride through woods accompanied by a Chinese mafoo. Chinese never hurt anyone. The mafoo and I do not speak to one another because I can't speak Chinese and his English is limited to a few words, and after a while I forget his presence altogether and start to daydream.

I daydream about a very handsome young man whom we see dining alone. He is swarthy and looks as if he could be a sheikh, like the sheikh of Araby on the record we used to have. I imagine him falling in love with me. I know it isn't even remotely possible, given my scrawny elbows and knees, but this does not deter me. In my daydream marvellous things happen. My eyes grow soft and dreamy, and possibly golden like those of the heroine in my South Pacific novel, though I have never seen such a wonder in a real human being. My hair turns red and falls in curls to my shoulders. I flesh out. My donkey becomes a horse. The mystery man in the dining-room has gone for a walk in the woods. We are about to meet. My mount stumbles and the ribbon of magic snaps.

The mafoo, the donkey and I reach the top of the hill and see the dunes that stretch away to the northeast and are small harbingers of the mighty Gobi that lies somewhere miles beyond the horizon. I am overcome by the vastness of the world and by its utter strangeness.

When I get home we all change and go in to dinner. I steal glances at the swarthy man on the opposite side of the room, blushing madly if he looks our way, which he does quite often, but on the way out we pass a full length mirror in the hall and one glance at my skinny frame, and hair scraggy from sun and brine, dissolves my ill-founded embarrassment. Later that night, I look out of the window and see Nina and my hero loitering by the garden gate. I settle down with Macaulay's Lays of Ancient Rome, an assignment for my Senior Cambridge examinations.

One day friends invite us to a kaoliang gruel lunch. They tell us it's the staple food of the north and is delicious. We stroll along the dusty country roads, hot with sun and sweet with the scent of roadside flowers, to their bungalow.

When I am served the gruel my anticipation turns to dismay. The kaoliang is appalling. I glance at Nina and she grimaces at me over the top of her bowl, but she continues eating, bravely and determinedly. Nina lives by my Aunt Lena's code of politeness. Our hosts gobble up their own bowlfuls. I follow Nina's example and push the mush down. I hope I don't throw up. I haven't eaten anything so awful since my days at my old school. My relief is great when dessert is served.

That night we are wakened by a commotion. The doctor is ill. He is in great pain. One of the servants is sent for the local physician. I wonder if it's the kaoliang. I lie in bed and sweat. What will happen to us if my uncle dies? I have never thought of him as being subject to the laws of mortality. I am suddenly once again overcome with the knowledge of our frailty. If a person as dependable as my uncle can become so ill, what hope is there for any of us? I experience a resurgence of my twelve-year-old anxiety about my mother. I wish I had never come on this holiday. There's nothing I long for so much as to have my mother's arms around me. I hear the arrival of the local doctor. After a long time Nina returns looking pale and bleary-eyed. "Is he going to be all right?" I ask. Nina shrugs disconsolately. "Was it the kaoliang?" I wonder. She doesn't know, she says, but after a while she adds that she wouldn't be surprised, it was truly awful. She smiles a little, but her eyes are worried.

We lie in bed in silence. The sounds outside die down. The night presses down on me with all the weight of prophetic doom. I think I shall never sleep again. I fall asleep.

In the morning my uncle is much better. We go to the beach without him, but in the evening, after tea, he joins us in our walk. I am relieved and happy and the imminence of my mother's demise fades.

One night my uncle summons us out just as we're about to go to bed. He tells us that here in the north, August is the month for shooting stars.

We watch, and soon we see the stars shoot across the skies, one after another. They leave a trail of brightness, like comets. Entranced, we cry out upon every manifestation. My neck aches from holding my head back, from straining to see every part of the heavens at the same time. The stars are very large and bright and I feel I could touch them if I could just reach a little higher.

After this we go out every night to see the shooting stars. One night we count 64. Then suddenly the show is over. The skies return to their normal impassivity.

Our stay at Peitaiho is coming to an end. We are now going on to Peking. I know that none of my friends has ever been to Peking. This time *I* will have something to talk about.

We board another train. I'm wearing my travelling-dress, my white broad-brimmed hat, my socks and my flat shoes. Nina wears a silk dress, silk stockings and high-heeled shoes. She looks very elegant. I'm not surprised that the sheikh chose to talk to her in the moonlight instead of me. I giggle.

We arrive at the Hotel de Wagon-Lits in Peking in the afternoon. We have two spacious rooms. My Aunt Lena orders afternoon tea and it arrives on a trolley with delicious little sandwiches and hot buttered scones in a covered silver salver. Nobody eats as much as I do. Aunt Lena laughs and says it's good for me, I'm much too skinny. She's right. I have no qualms about finishing everything off. Maybe I'll flesh out. But will my eyes turn golden?

Later in the evening we go down to dinner. Everything in the dining-room gleams and glitters. The table groans with cut glass and silverware. The tablecloths are shimmering white and stiff. I feel ill at ease and don't know what to order from the big menu, which is printed in French. It has several pages tied by an elegant cord. Nina sees my difficulty and helps me. Nina can read French easily.

The next day after breakfast we board rickshaws and go out to see the wonders of Peking. We are taken to the Forbidden City. Leaving our rickshaws behind we walk through a series of huge tunnels in enormously thick walls. These walls protected the residences of the Son of Heaven, as the Chinese emperor was called, and his family. Each tunnel in turn opens out onto a broad, sunny courtyard with dozens of small houses in which the Emperor's servants and retinue lived, quartered in order of their importance and relationship to his royal person. At last we find ourselves in what used to be the hideaway of the emperors of China.

Everywhere we look are tiled, curving roofs, broad marble staircases, huge stone temple dogs, gilded bronze lions, gigantic incense burners, carvings, fretwork, paintings, brilliant colours. We cross a moat spanned by five marble bridges and my uncle tells us that this moat is called the Golden Water Stream, though it doesn't appear very golden to me. He also tells us that the Forbidden City, the Ming tombs and the Temple of Heaven, which we will visit later, were all built by the third Ming Emperor whose name was Yong Le. The marble bridges, he says, were curved, so that they would look like the bows of the Tartars. I file all this information away in my memory bank.

We visit halls and pavilions and chambers. The reception hall is vast and I picture it filled with the guests or suppliants of the emperors in their rustly silks and brocades and with their long pigtails. We see huge ivory carvings and a room of mirrors. At one point I stand between two opposing mirrors and see an infinity of reflections of myself in my blue dress, white sunhat, socks and flat shoes. I wish I looked more elegant for the benefit of infinity. We see a famous old waterclock in the next room, sculptured jade and Ming vases.

We ride around Peking on the ancient wall that surrounds the city. We visit the Ming tombs and the Temple of Heaven, the open-air Altar of Heaven where the emperor made sacrifices to the gods, and the Summer Palace. In the Temple of Rain, Nina whispers into a circular wall and I hear her quite clearly at the opposite side. It is a miracle of ancient science.

The Temple of Heaven is round and has three tiered roofs tiled in blue. The top roof is crowned with a large gold knob like the knob on a sugar bowl cover. Marble terraces and staircases circle the building. There is a ramp in the centre of each staircase, carved with dragons and cranes and what look like giant snails but turn out to be clouds. When the emperor took one of his trips to the temple he was carried over the ramps in his sedan chair and if one of the carriers so much as touched the ramp he was instantly executed. I keep away from the ramps in case some spirit of illwill might still be lingering around them. Inside the temple, which is mysteriously dim, I see a dragon on the ceiling and elaborate decorations wherever I look. We stare at the gods in their niches and we smell incense burning.

I am mesmerized by the gods. I know that these gods are heathen and don't exist at all, but I can't help feeling that the beliefs of the Chinese people must be rooted in some worthwhile meaning, just as the beliefs of our churches find their meaning in the life and death of Jesus of Nazareth. I wonder why we are so scornful of the Chinese beliefs. The ancient images of the gods have a powerful effect on me, brooding, haunting, something like the icons in Aunt Lena's house. I don't mention this to anyone.

My uncle is interested in the architecture. He points out the amazing size of the supporting pillars. Nina and I stand on either side of one of the pillars and try to join hands, but we come nowhere close to reaching each other.

In the Summer Palace we cross a large lake full of water lilies by means of a seventeen-arch bridge. We visit a lavish marble boat, built by an improvident empress. I wonder if she was anything like Maria Mikhailovna. The boat juts out into the lake and now features a tea concession, but my Aunt Lena distrusts the purveyors of the refreshments so we pass up the tea. We follow an endless covered walkway on the shore of the lake, a gallery of pictures painted on overhead cross beams. As the beams are only a few feet apart and the walkway about half a mile long, there are hundreds of paintings. I imagine the emperors of China taking their evening strolls in their crusty robes, admiring the skill of the artists.

Back at the hotel, in the evening after dinner a Chinese magician performs in the lounge, holding us fascinated. As a finale, he appears in a black gown, lies down, rolls around on the floor and then produces five goldfish bowls, full of water and fish, from out of the folds of his gown. He invites us to test the water. I run up to put my finger in a bowl. The water's real all right. The goldfish swim around very happily.

The next day we go shopping in a special section of the city where the shops offer linens and curios. The interiors smell old and musty and the streets between these shops are narrow and dirty, and strung with banners. My Aunt Lena pokes around among the treasures looking for bargains. She buys some linens. Nina looks at the jade. It's very expensive so I put it out of my mind and buy my mother a small carved redwood box showing a couple under a canopy of trees, and a gold-lacquered bowl for my sister.

At last our holiday is over. Tomorrow we are taking the train from Peking back to Shanghai. It is called The Blue Express.

In the morning we pile into taxis with our luggage and drive to the station. Goodbye Wagon-Lits Hotel, goodbye Forbidden City, goodbye Summer Palace and Temple of Heaven, goodbye Peking, city of dreams, city of emperors, of wealth, of pride, of glory.

On the train I watch the countryside whizzing past.

When the train stops Chinese people climb off and on carrying large bundles and packages and baskets. They never have trunks or suitcases. Some of them carry wire containers holding live fowl. At every station my uncle hops out to take pictures. Both my aunt and I worry in case the train should leave without him. She stands at the top of the train steps calling to him not to go too far. He smiles and nods. He is eager to take pictures of the Chinese villages. My aunt shrugs scornfully at this notion, but I look at the black-tiled curving roofs, the peasants in their straw hats, the horned buffaloes, at the fields neatly divided to the horizon, at the canals and their willow trees, and I think I know how my uncle feels.

As I sit by the window I begin to think about everything I have seen. Although my father has often talked to me about the ancient civilization of China and quoted the famous quip about the Chinese reading newspapers with spectacles when we were eating each other without spectacles, I was never too impressed. But now the glories of the Chinese past occupy every corner of my mind, the grandeur and the cultural amenities of the ancient capital, the fervour of their religion, and, above all, the astonishing dexterity of their artists and craftsmen. The Chinese have been revealed to me in a light entirely different from the light in which Olga and I have been holding them. These are people to be admired and respected and wondered at, not people to be despised, to be forbidden entry into parks by notices that say: "No Chinese or dogs allowed." How did they become so dominated by hostile foreign powers, I wonder, their land commandeered, their people beggared? Names surface in my mind—Sun Yat-sen, Chiang Kai-shek; didn't someone called Mao Tse-tung organize a remarkable march into northern China encouraging the people on the way to stand up for their rights? Why do I know so little about all this?

I determine to listen more closely to my father to better my knowledge of this vast country. Did it not give us all sanctuary when we needed it? But how much do we care about it?

Our second night on the train is interrupted by great bangings and clangings and frenzied shouting, and our train is jerking and bumping. I am alarmed. My uncle tells us that we are about to cross the Yangtze River and that the train is being loaded on to a barge. We will be leaving our engine behind and will be attached to another engine on the other side.

The idea of loading a train and its passengers onto a barge in the middle of the night is pretty dismaying to me. How can anyone see what they are doing in the dark? Some uncertain lights are flickering outside but they don't look encouraging. Might not the train be misdirected and roll all of us into the Yangtsze River? We'd be trapped behind the mesh-covered windows.

I lie in my bunk and sweat. The train continues to bang and clang and jerk and bump. They're taking forever. Maybe they're making trial runs at the barge. Then suddenly there is silence. My uncle informs us that we're on the barge. He has been watching the whole operation with great interest. If it weren't so dark he'd be taking photographs. I can just hug my pillow and pray. We're crossing the river. Our compartment sways gently.

Suddenly there's a truly huge jerk and several thumps. This is it, I think, we've fallen off the barge, but my uncle cheerfully reports that we're across. We've made it.

My aunt gives thanks to God and then bids my uncle to come to bed. She sounds aggravated, as if he is somehow responsible for the foolhardy crossing.

We arrive back in Shanghai early in the morning. I'm longing to see my parents and my sister. I can't wait to describe my super vacation to Olga in every detail. This year when they ask us to write the usual essay about our summer holidays, I'll certainly have something to write about.

On the drive home I couldn't be happier. I haven't the

faintest suspicion of the forces lining up all around me to blight my arrival at adulthood. Totally unalerted as to what is actually taking place in China, I feel no trepidation. I do not know that within a short year I will witness events that will open the way for one of the most awesome capsizals in history, and that my young and bewildered self will be present on the actual stage now being set for those events as the play unfolds.